Series authors:
Malcolm Mann
Steve Taylore-Knowles

Laser A1+

Teacher's Book

MACMILLAN

Macmillan Education
4 Crinan Street
London N1 9XW
A division of Macmillan Publishers Limited
Companies and representatives throughout the world

ISBN 978-0-230-42465-4

Series authors: Malcolm Mann & Steve Taylore-Knowles

First published 2012

Original design by Peter Burgess
Page make-up by Expo Holdings, Malaysia
Illustrated by Red Giraffe
Cover design by Peter Burgess

The author and publishers would like to thank the following for permission to reproduce their photographs:

Bananastock; **Getty**; ImageSource; **Macmillan**/David Tolley; Rubber Ball; Up the Resolution.

Printed and bound in Thailand

2017 2016 2015
11 10 9 8 7 6

Contents

Introduction: Welcome to *Laser A1+*!

Laser A1+ Teacher's Book is designed to make your job as easy and stress-free as possible. To this end, it's worth spending a few minutes reading this introduction to see how the course is structured and what it provides you with in terms of materials.

We hope this Teacher's Book will be a useful tool for you throughout the teaching year. The more familiar you are with the various features that are included in the book, the more useful we think you will find it.

Components
A number of different components make up the *Laser A1+* course:

- *Laser A1+* **Student's Book** with **Student's CD-ROM**
- *Laser A1+* Student's Book **Class Audio CDs**
- *Laser A1+* **Workbook** (with and without key versions) with **Audio CD**
- *Laser A1+* **Teacher's Book**
- *Laser A1+* **Teacher's DVD-ROM** (packaged with the Teacher's Book)
- *Laser A1+* **Digibook** (packaged with the Teacher's Book)

Let's look at each of them in turn.

Laser A1+ Student's Book

- There are 14 topic-based units. Each unit contains the following sections:
  - **Get ready!:** developing key topic vocabulary in preparation for the reading text
  - **Reading:** developing key reading skills through the presentation of an attractively illustrated text
  - **Wordpower!:** focusing on topic-based lexis from the Reading section, this section seeks to build up students' lexical knowledge
  - **Grammar 1:** focusing on one key grammar point (which has been exemplified in the preceding Reading text), this section presents the grammar point and is followed by exercises for consolidation
  - a second **Wordpower!:** focusing on topic-based phrasal verbs, word formation, patterns, collocations, etc, again aimed at building up students' lexical repertoire
  - **Listening:** developing key listening skills through a variety of exercise types
  - **Speaking:** developing key speaking skills based on a variety of scenarios that have relevance in everyday life, and including a **Phrase Bank!**, feature which provides useful words and phrases through a functional structure
  - **SoundSpot:** focusing on the production and reception of key phonetic areas that may prove problematic for students
  - **Grammar 2:** focusing on a second key grammar point and again followed by exercises for consolidation
  - **Writing:** developing key writing skills through the study of model writing tasks and related exercises, and including a **Language Lab** feature, which focuses on the language and style required by specific writing types
  - **Plan your project!:** working towards the production of a piece of writing, this feature guides and supports the students towards completion of the writing task
- **Homework!** sections throughout the Student's Book indicate when and which Workbook exercises should be assigned.
- After every two units, there is a two-page **Revision** section, revising and consolidating the grammar and vocabulary from the preceding two units.
- At the back of the book, there is:
  - a 7-page **Writing database**, providing further models of all the writing types covered in the course, plus useful information on language, style and structure.
  - a 4-page alphabetical **Vocabulary database**, covering all the phrases, phrasal verbs, patterns, collocations and compound nouns covered in the course and providing example sentences for each one.
  - a 2-page **Speaking database** arranged by function, providing examples of all the key language required for the Speaking sections.
  - an 11-page **Grammar database**, containing additional information for each grammar point covered in the Student's Book, plus a Quick Check task to consolidate each grammar point.
  - a **Songs and Webquests** section, containing task-based songs for units 1–2, 5–6, 9–10, 13–14, and Webquests for units 3–4, 7–8, 11–12 and 1–14.

Laser A1+ Student's CD-ROM

- Every Student's Book includes a CD-ROM which gives students the opportunity to practise and develop their language learning in a motivating and enjoyable way. It contains nine additional revision and consolidation tasks for each unit:
  - 3 of these tasks focus on **vocabulary**.
  - 3 of these tasks focus on **grammar**.
  - 3 of these tasks focus on **language skills**.

- 1 or 2 of the above tasks in each unit require the students to carry out some form of **listening** activity.
- The Student's CD-ROM provides the opportunity for extra practice and consolidation of the structures and lexical items learned in the Student's Book units. It is a flexible component in that it can be used in class as an integrated part of the lesson, or can be used by students independently outside the classroom, either as a homework task or as an extra option to support their learning.

Laser A1+ Class Audio CDs

- These contain all the recorded material for the Speaking, SoundSpot and Listening sections of the Student's Book.
- The CD track references for this audio material are included in the Teacher's Book.

Laser A1+ Workbook

- There are two versions of the Workbook: one with answer key and one without.
- The Workbook revises and consolidates the work done in the Student's Book, and at times extends it further too.
- All Workbook exercises are designed so that they can be assigned for homework. The relevant exercises are clearly presented throughout the Student's Book, in the **Homework** boxes.
- Each unit of the Workbook contains the following sections:
  - **Reading:** consolidating and extending the work done in the Student's Book Reading section, using a variety of text types and exercises
  - **Wordpower!:** revising and consolidating the work done in the Student's Book first **Wordpower!** section
  - **Grammar 1:** revising and consolidating the work done in the Student's Book Grammar 1 section
  - **Wordpower!:** revising and consolidating the work done in the Student's Book second **Wordpower!** section
  - **Listening:** consolidating and extending the work done in the Student's Book Listening section, using a variety of listening situations and a range of speakers
  - **Grammar 2:** revising and consolidating the work done in the Student's Book Grammar 1 section
  - **Writing:** revising, consolidating and extending the work done in the Student's Book Writing section (up to and including **Language Lab**), using various exercises requiring students to understand and analyse pieces of text

- The Workbook also contains eight 1-page **Check your progress!** tests for units 1–2, 3–4, 5–6, 7–8, 9–10, 11–12, 13–14 and 1–14. Each of these is marked out of 25.
- The **Workbook Audio CD** contains all the recorded material for the Listening sections throughout the Workbook.

Laser A1+ Teacher's Book

- As we said earlier, this Teacher's Book has been specially written in order to make your life as a teacher easier. We have tried to include a range of useful information along with detailed teacher's notes for every Student's Book task. Once you have familiarised yourself with the Teacher's Book and you know what information it contains and where that information can be found, we hope you will find it constructive and helpful as you work your way through *Laser A1+* with your students.
- The Teacher's Book contains:
  - information on the **Target language** for each unit.
  - information on the **Aim** of each task and section.
  - detailed guidelines for teachers on how to use the material in the Student's Book most effectively, including what to write on the board in **On the Board** sections.
  - an **Answer key** to all exercises with additional explanation of answers where appropriate.
  - **Warm up!** and **Cool down!** tasks for each section, which lead into or out of the tasks in the Student's Book, often providing opportunities for the students to personalise what they have read or listened to, etc.
  - **Additional Task** boxes, containing suggestions for supplementary activities.
  - A **CD Track reference** for each listening activity.
  - **Homework!** sections indicating when and which Workbook exercises should be assigned.
  - The **audioscripts** for all listening activities in the Student's Book, where the complete script does not appear on the Student's Book page.
  - References to additional tasks and tests on the **Student's CD-ROM** and the **Teacher's DVD-ROM.**

- We recommend that, irrespective of whether you're a new or highly experienced teacher, you make the most of the material provided in the Teacher's

Book both during the planning of a lesson and, if appropriate, during the lesson itself.

- However, we do not want you to feel restrained by the notes and guidance in the Teacher's Book. You may wish to omit certain parts of an activity, or extend an activity further, or carry out an activity in a different way to the way suggested. You know your students and their needs best, and you know what the time constraints are. The aim of the Teacher's Book is to help you, not hinder you, in your teaching.

Laser A1+ Teacher's DVD-ROM

- This is packaged with the Teacher's Book and contains several extra resources which we hope you will find useful.
- There are three sections on the DVD-ROM: **Tests**, **Test Generator** and **Teacher's Support Videos**.

- The **Tests** section contains:
  - 14 **Unit Tests**, focusing on reading, grammar, vocabulary and writing
  - 3 **Term Tests**, covering units 1-5, 6-10 and 11-14
  - 1 **Final Test**, covering units 1-14
  - **The Answer key** for all the tests

- All the tests are available as either editable Word documents or as PDFs. If you opt for the Word documents, you can change or add to the material as many times as you like in order to make it suitable for your particular student group. If you opt for the PDFs, the tests are formatted and ready for you to print and use immediately. But you won't be able to edit the tests in PDF format.

- The **Test Generator** section allows you to produce custom-made tests, and contains the following elements for each unit:
  - 6 **Vocabulary** tasks
  - 6 **Grammar** tasks
  - 4 **Reading** tasks
  - 3 **Speaking** tasks
  - 4 **Listening** tasks
  - The **Answer key** for all the tasks

- The **Test Generator** enables you to select the specific skills you wish to test, choosing as few or as many as you like. It also enables you to choose which unit or units you would like to test at any one time.
- Approximately half of the **Test Generator** tasks in each unit are labelled as being **less challenging** and the other half as **more challenging**, allowing you to choose appropriate tasks for particular students or groups of students depending on their level and ability.
- Many of the tasks included in the bank of **Test Generator** material are good preparation for KET tasks.

- The **Teacher's Support Videos** section of the DVD-ROM contains a series of short videos featuring both the *Laser* authors (Malcolm Mann and Steve Taylore-Knowles).
- The aim of the videos is to provide teachers with a range of suggestions and ideas about how to use the material in *Laser A1+*.
- The topics covered in *Laser A1+* **Teacher's Support Videos** are:
  - **Introduction**
  - **Vocabulary:** Using the vocabulary database
  - **Listening:** Using songs
  - **Speaking:** Using speaking models
  - **Writing:** Developing writing skills
  - **Grammar:** Presenting grammar
  - **Reading:** Reading for gist and specific information

- In the videos, the authors explain the rationale behind some of the features in *Laser A1+* Student's Book, suggest procedures for working through the *Laser A1+* material or give ideas for more ways of exploiting the Student's Book material.
- Each video is between three and four minutes long.

Laser A1+ Digibook

- The **Digibook** is a page-faithful, digital version of the Student's Book.
- The *Laser* **Digibook** contains the **Interactive Book** with embedded **Audio** throughout. The **Digibook** are designed for you to use in class. To use the book, you will need a computer connected to a projector, or an Interactive White Board (IWB). However, for those of you who are not familiar with IWB techniques, it is important to remember that the **Digibook** is very simple to use and requires no previous IWB experience whatsoever. You will be able to see the relevant icons for audio material, answer keys and links to the grammar database explanations, as well as the zoom feature enabling you to enlarge specific exercises or areas of the Student's Book page.
- The **Digibook** contains a full answer key to all tasks. Answers for each individual exercise can be revealed as and when you feel it's appropriate.
- All the **Audio** material featured in the Student's Book, including songs and all listening exercises, is embedded in the **Digibook** and can be played by clicking on the relevant listening icon.
- The **Digibook** can provide a visual focal point for your lesson and enable more 'heads-up' learning, where your students are much more engaged and are all focusing on the Student's Book pages as projected at the front of the classroom rather than all working with their heads down, reading the book on their desks. This makes the class more cohesive. You can consolidate new vocabulary, demonstrate exercises,

play audio tracks, and check answers to exercises. You can also personalise the content, adapting it to your own teaching style, by writing, highlighting and drawing on the pages using the optional IWB tools provided.

We very much hope you and your students enjoy using *Laser A1+* as much as we enjoyed writing it. If you or your students have any questions about the course, please contact us through the publisher. We would love to hear from you!

Have a great school year!

Malcolm Mann & Steve Taylore-Knowles

Student's Book contents map

Unit	Reading	Wordpower! (1)	Grammar 1	Wordpower! (
1 This is Me! PAGE 6	reading for gist / specific information (multiple matching, multiple choice questions)	topic vocabulary	*be, have/have got*	general basic vocabulary (family members)
2 On the Farm! PAGE 14	reading for gist / specific information (matching headings to paragraphs, comprehension questions)	topic vocabulary	present simple	general basic vocabulary (time)
3 Going Shopping! PAGE 24	reading for gist / specific information (multiple matching, T/F)	topic vocabulary	present continuous	general basic vocabulary (size and shape)
4 Read All About It! PAGE 32	reading for gist / specific information (T/F, match questions and answers)	topic vocabulary	question words	general basic vocabulary (ways of talking)
5 The Travel Bug! PAGE 42	reading for gist / specific information (multiple matching, sentence completion)	topic vocabulary	past simple - basic irregular verbs *(was/were, had, went, took, did, made, got)*	general basic vocabulary (countries)
6 Animal Magic! PAGE 50	reading for gist / specific information (matching to make questions, T/F/DS)	topic vocabulary	regular and irregular plurals	general basic vocabulary (ways of moving)
7 At the Airport! PAGE 60	reading for gist / specific information (multiple matching, T/F)	topic vocabulary	countable and uncountable nouns	general basic vocabulary (materials)

Listening	Speaking	SoundSpot	Grammar 2	Writing
listening for gist / specific information (T/F, sentence completion)	talking about yourself	pronunciation of final *s*	possessives	personal profile
listening for gist / specific information (multiple matching, multiple choice)	talking about daily activities	pronunciation – tongue twister with *s* and *sh*	adverbs of frequency	informal email (1)
listening for gist / specific information (multiple choice – pictures, sentence completion)	talking about what people are doing at the moment	pronunciation of similar sounding words	pronouns	description of a picture of people
listening for gist / specific information (multiple choice, sentence completion)	asking and answering questions (1)	pronunciation of question words	*too* and *very*	interview (dialogue) (1)
listening for gist / specific information (multiple matching, sentence completion)	talking about past events	stress in names of countries	past simple – regular verbs and more irregular verbs	blog post (1)
listening for gist / specific information (multiple matching, text completion)	giving simple instructions	stress in 2- or 3-syllable words	articles	note (giving instructions)
listening for gist / specific information (multiple choice questions, sentence completion)	agreeing and disagreeing	pronunciation of hard and soft *g*	quantitative adjectives (*some, any, many, much, a lot of, no*)	description of a scene

Unit	Reading	Wordpower (1)	Grammar 1	Wordpower (2)
8 **Lucky Escapes!** PAGE 68	reading for gist / specific information (multiple matching, *yes/no* questions)	topic vocabulary	past continuous	general basic vocabulary (gestures)
9 **Friends and Family!** PAGE 78	reading for gist / specific information (multiple matching, T/F)	topic vocabulary	*can* for ability and requests; *could* for requests	general basic vocabulary (feelings)
10 **Being the Best!** PAGE 86	reading for gist / specific information (multiple choice questions, sentence completion)	topic vocabulary	comparatives	general basic vocabulary (appearance)
11 **Planning for Tomorrow!** PAGE 96	reading for gist / specific information (multiple matching, questions)	topic vocabulary	*be going to* for future plans	general basic vocabulary (quantity)
12 **Lights! Camera! Action!** PAGE 104	reading for gist / specific information (matching questions multiple choice questions)	topic vocabulary	present continuous for future arrangements	general basic vocabulary (places)
13 **Raising Money!** PAGE 114	reading for gist / specific information (multiple matching, T/F)	topic vocabulary	present perfect simple *(ever/never)*	general basic vocabulary (position)
14 **Looking Ahead!** PAGE 122	reading for gist / specific information (matching pictures and paragraphs, selecting statements)	topic vocabulary	first conditional	general basic vocabulary (directions)

Listening	Speaking	SoundSpot	Grammar 2	Writing
listening for gist / specific information (multiple matching, multiple choice questions)	telling simple stories	similar sounding words	short answer forms	story
listening for gist / specific information (multiple choice questions, identifying speakers)	asking for, giving and refusing permission	*can / can't*	*should* for advice; *must* and *have to* for obligation	set of household rules
listening for gist / specific information (multiple choice questions –pictures, comprehension questions)	making comparisons	sounds of letter *o*	superlatives	description (comparing people's appearance)
listening for gist / specific information (multiple matching, sequencing information)	talking about future plans	words and phrases for quantity	*will* for future facts	informal email (2)
listening for gist / specific information (multiple matching, T/F)	talking about future arrangements	pronunciation of the word endings *-or, -er, -a*	prepositions of time and place	interview (dialogue) (2)
listening for gist / specific information (multiple matching, multiple choice questions)	asking and answering questions (2)	pronunciation of the word ending *-ed*	adverbs of manner	blog post (2)
listening for gist / specific information (identifying information, drawing a route from information given)	talking about future possibilities	pronunciation of *gh*	adverbs of degree	article

1

This is Me!

Target language

Reading skills: reading for gist / specific information (multiple matching, multiple choice questions)
Vocabulary: topic vocabulary (talking about yourself and your friends, family members)
Grammar: *be, have/have got*, possessives
Listening skills: listening for gist / specific information (T/F, sentence completion)
Speaking skills: talking about yourself
Pronunciation skills: pronunciation of final *s*
Writing skills: personal profile

Get ready!

Aim: to learn and identify words and phrases to talk about yourself and your friends

- Ask students to look at the pictures and describe what they can see, eg two babies (pictures 1 and 2), a cat, a dog and a bird (picture 3), the world (picture 4), houses/buildings/a town (picture 5).
- Give students a short time to match each word or phrase with the pictures.
- You may also wish to refer students to the *Vocabulary database* on page 139.
- Check answers orally and write the numbers of the pictures on the board along with the correct letter and word or phrase for each picture.

1 b	2 e	3 d	4 a	5 c

Reading

Aim: to give practice in reading for gist and specific information in texts in which young people are talking about themselves, their family and their friends

Warm up!

Aim: to introduce the concept of personal profiles

- Write the following prompts on the board and check students know what they mean.

ON THE BOARD

Name:
Age:
Town:
Family members:
Friends' names:
Pets:
Likes:

- Ask students to write down the prompts in their notebooks. Then go through each of the prompts and answer them orally with your own information using words and not complete sentences, eg *Name: Paula/ John, Age: 26, Town: London, Family members: mum – Fran, dad – Stephen, sister – Sarah,* etc. For 'Likes', make sure students understand that this means things they like such as computer games or books.
- Ask students to complete each of the items with their own information.

1

- Ask students to silently and individually read the personal profiles. Encourage them to ignore all unknown vocabulary at this stage.
- Ask students some very general and simple questions about the profiles, eg *Who are the writers?* (Harry Lee, Anna Melnik, Sunil Mittal, Joe Anderson), *What are the profiles about?* (their lives).
- Give students a few minutes to do exercise 1. Go round the class helping students where necessary.
- Check answers orally and/or by writing them on the board.

	Brothers	Sisters
Harry	✗	✓
Anna	✗	✗
Sunil	✓	✓
Joe	✗	✗

2

- Encourage students to do this task quickly but carefully (to help develop their scanning skills).
- Explain to students they should decide which answer, A, B or C, is correct for each question.
- Encourage students to underline in the text where they find the answer.
- When they have finished, discuss the answers together. Encourage students to justify their answers by giving reasons.

1 B (She hasn't got a name! She's just 'cat'!)
2 B (My family has a house in the country and I often spend time there with Anastasia and Oksana.)
3 C (My favourite brother Sachin has got a job in Delhi and he lives there, but the rest of us live together in Mumbai.)
4 A (…we live in a small town in Ohio, so it can get a bit lonely.)

3

- Write the names *Harry*, *Anna*, *Sunil* and *Joseph* on the board and ask students to say who they want to be friends with and give some reasons why they would want to be friends with them.
- Encourage students to use complete sentences when answering. Write brief notes under each heading according to what the students tell you.
- Ask students to write their choices and reasons why in their Student's Book.
- Go round the class helping students where necessary.

Cool down!

Aim: to encourage students to talk about differences

- Ask students to look at the four personal profiles again.
- Ask students to talk about things from the profiles that are different to their own lives, eg *Anna's in the 8th Grade, but I'm in the 6th Grade. Sunil has got a large family, but I've got a small family. Joe lives in a small town, but I live in a big town.*
- You may wish to point out to students that how people talk about school years varies depending on where they live, eg in the UK they talk about Year 7, for example, and in the USA they talk about 7th Grade.

Wordpower!

Aim: to develop students' topic vocabulary

- Explain to students that all the answers appear in the personal profiles they have read.
- Ask students to try to complete the gaps without referring back to the text, but explain that they can if necessary.
- Remind students that they should only write one letter in each gap and that the first letter has been given to help them.
- Encourage them to be careful with their spelling.
- You may also wish to refer students to the *Vocabulary database* on page 139.
- Check the answers orally by asking students to read out the questions.

1 best	3 country	5 chat online
2 close	4 share	6 only

HOMEWORK!

Assign exercises 1–3 on pages 4 and 5 of the Workbook.

Grammar 1 G

be, have/have got

Aim: to facilitate students' understanding of the functions and usage of the verbs be and *have/have got*

Warm up!

Aim: to describe what things and people are like and to talk about what they possess

- Write the following words on the board:

ON THE BOARD

MY FRIEND:
ANNA
13
A SISTER
NO PETS

- Ask students to talk about Anna as if she were their friend, eg *My friend is Anna. or My friend's name is Anna. She's 13 years old. She has/has got a sister. She doesn't have/hasn't got a pet/any pets.*

Grammar presentation 1

- Go through the grammar presentation with students. Check they understand how and when we use *be* and *have/have got* (to describe things and to say what things are ours, respectively).
- Explain to students that there is more information on *be* and *have/have got* in *Grammar database 1* on page 145 at the back of the book.

- Ask them to read through the information in the Grammar database on their own.
- Ask them if they have any questions.
- Ask students to complete the Quick check task on page 145.
- Check answers orally and ask students to justify their answers, eg *1 I have a brother.* because *I* takes *have*.

Quick check

Circle these correct answers:

1 have	4 Yes, I have.
2 Yes, I am.	5 No, they aren't.
3 hasn't got	

1

- Explain to students that they have to choose the correct form of either *be* or *have/have got* in each of these sentences.
- Check answers orally and/or by writing them on the board.

1 is	4 Do	7 Have
2 are	5 don't	8 hasn't
3 has	6 has	

2

- Ask students to look at the pictures and say if they don't know what any of these pictures are.
- Ask students to tick which items they've got and write complete sentences below. Encourage them to write negative sentences about the items that they haven't got.
- Check answers orally and/or by writing them on the board.

3

- Explain to students that you're going to ask them who has got each one of the items from exercise 2. Ask students to raise their hand if they've got the item that you're asking them about.
- Copy the following chart on the board (but you may have to adjust the numbers, depending on your class size).

ON THE BOARD

- Under the chart, draw a picture of the item that you are asking students about. Alternatively, you can write the word.
- Place a mark on the board that represents how many students have got that particular item.
- Ask students to place marks on the charts in their Student's Book as you go along with the exercise.
- Discuss the results of the survey. Ask students to tell the class what items they have that other students have or don't have, eg *I have a skateboard, but John doesn't have a skateboard. Mark has a watch, but I haven't got a watch.*

Additional Task

- You may wish students to carry out a second class survey, where students go round the room asking other students what they have.
- You could encourage students to come up with different things to ask about, such as DVD player, rollerskates, comic books, sunglasses, guitar, hamster, camera, clock etc.
- After they have carried out their survey, students can report back orally to the whole class on their findings, and/or write sentences giving the results of their survey, eg *12 students in my class have got a watch.*

Cool down!

Aim: to review the functions and usage of *be* and *have/have* got

- Ask students to talk about their friends or family members. Ask them to say their names and how old they are, eg *My best friend's name is George and he is 13 years old.*
- Encourage them to make statements to say what their friends or family members have got that they haven't got and vice versa, eg *My best friend Alice has got an MP3 player, but I haven't got an MP3 player. I've got a mobile phone, but my brother hasn't got a mobile phone.*

HOMEWORK!

Assign exercises 1–4 on pages 5 and 6 of the Workbook.

Wordpower!

Aim: to develop students' ability to recognise and use words related to family members

1

- Ask students to look at the family tree, then read the text and choose a word from the box to go in each gap.
- Encourage students to make a guess if they're not sure.
- You may also wish to refer students to the *Vocabulary database* on page 139.
- Check the answers orally and/or write answers on the board.

1 aunt	6 grandfather
2 uncle	7 grandmother
3 niece	8 great-grandfather
4 cousin	9 great-grandmother
5 nephew	

Additional Task

- Using the other pictures in the family tree, ask students to say how the different people may be related to other people in the family, eg *Arthur is Toby and Sam's grandfather, and he's Alice's father.*

2

- Ask students to draw their own family tree using the family tree in exercise 1 as guide. Go round the class helping students where necessary.
- Ask students to form pairs and ask each other about their families.

HOMEWORK!

Assign exercises 1 and 2 on page 7 of the Workbook.

Listening

Aim: to give practice in listening for gist and specific information

Warm up!

Aim: to introduce the topic of radio shows

- Ask students to look at the sentences in exercise 1.
- Ask simple questions about the sentences and elicit responses, eg *Who are the people in the radio show?* (Paula, Seb and Sienna), *What is the radio show about?* (Their families and their rooms)

1

- Explain to students that they are going to listen to people talking on a radio show.
- Go through the list and ask students to predict what the caller might say for each thing, eg *I've got a large family.* or *I haven't got a large family.* for *Paula has got a large family.*
- Explain to students that they will hear all three people in the show.
- Ask students to circle true (T) or false (F) as they listen to the show.
- Play the CD track once all the way through. Repeat if necessary.

1 F (I'm an only child,...)
2 T (I've got a lot of books and CDs, and I have pictures on the walls. ...I've got a computer.)
3 T (...there's me, my brother and my sisters... And my four grandparents and two great-grandparents. ... And there are aunts and uncles and some cousins.)
4 F (I share with my brother.)
5 T (I love our dog, Prince.)
6 T (It's large, and it's full of my things.)

CD Track 1

2

- Explain to students that they will listen to the recording again.
- Ask them to read through the sentences before they listen, and to predict the answers.
- You may wish to check at this point that students understand the meaning of the word relatives in number 1.
- Play the CD again. Pause when you hear the first correct answer (*an only child*), and ask students to write it in the gap. Check their answers.
- Play the rest of the recording in its entirety and ask students to listen and work independently to fill in the rest of the answers.
- Check answers together with students. If necessary, play the recording again for students to check incorrect answers.

1 an only child	4 fish
2 a TV	5 grandparents
3 great-grandparents	6 best friend

CD Track 1

3

- Ask students to form pairs and ask and answer the questions from the exercise. When one of the students has asked all the questions, they should swap roles.
- Encourage students to think of other questions to ask and answer each other, eg *Have you got a computer at home? Do you use the computer to talk to people? Have you got any grandparents? Do they live with you? Do you see them often?*

Cool down!

Aim: to personalise what the students have listened to

- Ask students to say how their lives are similar or different to Paula's, Seb's or Sienna's, eg *Paula is an only child, but I've got two brothers.*

HOMEWORK!

Assign exercises 1 and 2 on pages 7 and 8 of the Workbook.

Speaking

Aim: to provide practice in talking about yourself and describing other people

Warm up!

Aim: to introduce students to basic phrases we use to talk about ourselves and others

- Choose a student and ask the other students to describe that student's hair, eg *Mike's got short hair.* or *Paul's got very short hair.* Choose another student whose hair is different and ask the other students to describe that student's hair, eg *Maria's got very long hair.*

- Encourage students to use *has/has got* in their answers (or *have/have got* if you ask students to describe two students at the same time).

1

- Ask students to look at the pictures and match each word or phrase with the pictures. Remind students that all of the pictures match with more than one word or phrase.
- When they have finished, check the answers orally, and/or write them on the board.

1 d	3 a	5 c	7 a
2 b	4 c	6 b	8 d

2

- Ask students to complete the profile using their own information.
- You may wish to encourage them to add any additional information that they think is interesting.

3

- Go through the *Phrase Bank!* with students before you ask students to do exercise 3.
- Point out that we use these words and phrases to talk about ourselves.
- You may also wish to refer students to the *Speaking database* on page 143.
- Ask students to use their notes from exercise 2 and the phrases in the *Phrase Bank!* to tell the class about themselves.

Cool down!

Aim: to give students additional practice talking about themselves and others

- Ask a student to choose a friend, a family member or another student in class and talk about what is similar, eg *I'm very tall and my friend Jim is tall too.* and what is different, eg *I've got two sisters, but my friend Helen is an only child.*

SoundSpot

Aim: to give practice in pronouncing the final *s*

1

- Check that students know the word *sound.*
- Ask students to look at the seven words and guess how we say the *s* at the end of each of the words.
- Encourage them to say the words aloud, but don't correct their pronunciation or answers at this stage.
- Play the recording and then check students' answers.
- Point out that sometimes we pronounce the *s* at the end of a word like a 'z'.
- You may wish to ask students if they can think of other words (eg *laptops, talks*) with the same *s* sound as *aunts* and *pets.*

	like 's'	like 'z'
1 aunts	✓	
2 brothers		✓
3 cousins		✓
4 friends		✓
5 pets	✓	
6 sisters		✓
7 uncles		✓

CD Track 2

2

- Ask students to look at the sentences and say each of them aloud, but don't correct their pronunciation.
- Play the recording and ask students if they pronounced the sentences correctly or if they need to practise again.

CD Track 3

Additional Task

- Ask students to practise with some other words, such as cats, dogs, things, rooms, bicycles, rabbits, etc.
- Encourage students to work out individually or in pairs which words have a final *s* that does not sound like a 'z' (the ones that end in *ts*).

Grammar 2 G

Possessives
Aim: to facilitate students' understanding of the function and use of possessives

Warm up!

Aim: to talk about things that belong to people (possessives)

- Write on the board:

ON THE BOARD

I've got a pen. It's ..... pen. It's ..... .
You've got a book. It's ..... book. It's ..... .

- Ask students to look at the sentences on the board. Say the first sentence in the first line aloud, *I've got a pen.* Then ask students if they can complete the second and third sentences on the first line.
- Continue to the second line and ask students to say the second and third sentences. Then call on students to come up with their own sentences about themselves and their classmates, eg *I've got a schoolbag. It's my schoolbag. It's mine. You've got a rubber. It's your rubber. It's yours.*
- You may wish to make this a game where if a student gets it right, they can choose another student to come up with the next sentences.

Grammar presentation 2

- Go through the grammar presentation with students. Check they understand when we use possessives (to show that something belongs to someone).
- Explain to students that there is more information in *Grammar database 2* on page 146 at the back of the book.
- Ask them to read through the information in the *Grammar database* on their own.
- Ask them if they have any questions.
- Ask students to complete the Quick check task on page 146.
- Check answers orally and ask students to justify their answers, eg *1 That's my desk.* because we use possessive adjectives before nouns.

Quick check

Circle these correct answers:
1 my
2 its
3 John's
4 hers
5 girls'

1

- Ask students to read the sentences and, using the word in bold, complete each gap with the correct possessive.
- When students have finished, check the answers together orally.

1 your	3 our	5 my
2 their	4 his	6 her

2

- Ask students to complete the exercise by putting the words of each sentence in order and using *'s* or *s'* where appropriate.
- Check answers by asking students to write them on the board.

2 My sister's pet rabbit hasn't got a name.
3 Other people's families are interesting.
4 Theo's mum hasn't got brothers or sisters.
5 Has Imogen's family got a large house?
6 My brothers' room is next to mine.

3

- Ask students to complete the exercise by replacing the word in bold with the correct word.
- When students have finished, play the recording to check the answers together.
- Assign students to read out the dialogue. Time permitting, repeat with as many students as possible.

1 mine	5 hers	8 my
2 my	6 David's	9 his
3 his	7 yours	10 our
4 mine		

CD Track 4

Cool down!

Aim: to review the functions and usage of possessives

- Ask students to look around the classroom and say which items belong to whom, eg *That bag is Lydia's bag. It's her bag. It's hers.* or *That desk is the teacher's desk. It's your desk. It's yours.* or *That board is our board. It's ours.*
- Encourage students to use both possessive adjectives, the possessive form of nouns, and possessive pronouns to talk about as many things in the classroom as they can.

HOMEWORK!

Assign exercises 1–4 on pages 8 and 9 of the Workbook.

Writing

Aim: to develop the skills necessary to produce a personal profile

Warm up!

Aim: to further develop students' understanding of personal profiles

- Ask students if they have ever read a profile about a person in a magazine or on a website such as Facebook.
- Ask students what personal information they read about these people, eg their age, where they live, where they are from, what they like and don't like.
- Accept all suggestions at this point, but allow students to disagree with each other if they want to.

1

- Ask students to read the profile silently and individually, and then to answer the questions, deciding if the statements are true (T) or false (F).
- Check answers together when students have finished.

1 F	2 F	3 F	4 T

2

- Explain the meaning of the phrase 'in common' if students are not familiar with it (having shared interests/characteristics/etc).
- Ask students to write what they have in common with Zara.
- Go round the classroom to assist students where necessary.
- Call on students to tell the class what they have in common with Zara.

3

- Ask students to read the personal profile again and match each paragraph with a statement.
- Check answers together when students have finished.

1 b	2 c	3 a	4 d

Language Lab

Aim: to focus on key language skills required to achieve this kind of writing task

- Ask students to read the statements aloud.
- Check their understanding of terminology such as 'short forms', 'exclamation marks', etc before they attempt the task.
- You may wish students to find and underline the examples individually, or to work together as a class.

1. I'm Zara and I'm 13 years old. / I'm quite tall. I've got … And I've got / That's what / I've got a large family. I've got … and we're very close. / We don't have many cousins / we've got our own friends / but it's a large room so that's OK. I've got a desk / it's got / I've got / I've also got lots of photos / It's full of excitement and magic!
2. I'm Zara
3. That's what my friends say, anyway! / Over the desk I've got pictures of my favourite bands and film stars! I've also got lots of photos of me and my sisters! / My favourite film star is Jennifer Aniston because her films are always very funny! / It's full of excitement and magic!
4. See paragraph breaks in text.

Cool down!

Aim: to personalise what the students have just read

- Ask students if they would like to meet Zara.
- Encourage them to give reasons why they would or wouldn't like to.
- Ask them what other things they would like to know about Zara. Encourage them to think of questions they would ask her, eg *Where are you from? Do you like school? What do you like about school? What don't you like about it? What other film stars do you like?* etc.

HOMEWORK!

Assign exercise 1 on page 9 of the Workbook.

Plan your project!

Aim: to guide students through the writing process

1

- Explain to students that they are going to write a personal profile similar to Zara's.
- Ask students to write two sentences about themselves in order to introduce themselves and describe what they look like.

2

- Explain to students that they are going to make a list of some of their favourite things.
- Ask students to make short notes about why they like these things.
- Go round the classroom to assist students where necessary.

3

- Explain to students that they are going to complete the *Planner*.
- Point to the first column and explain that these are the different parts of the profile.
- Point to the second column and explain that this is useful information about each part.
- Ask the students to complete the notes in the third column with information about themselves.
- Encourage them to use their imagination.
- Check their planners before moving on to exercise 4.

4

- You may wish to assign this for homework or, if there's time, for the students to do this in class.
- Explain to students that they are going to use their notes from the *Planner* in exercise 3 to write their profile.
- Explain to them that using their notes is important for making a detailed plan before they start writing.
- Allow them to look back at Zara's personal profile if they're not sure what to do. At this stage, the most important thing is that the students create a successful piece of writing.
- You may also wish them to consult the *Writing database* on page 133, which has a further model to study.
- You may wish to encourage stronger students to take risks with their writing, but it's probably best if weaker students follow the model completely.
- Encourage the students to add photos or drawings to their profile to make it look more authentic.
- You may wish to comment on the students' writing before they produce a final version.

Additional Tasks and Tests

- Student's CD-ROM: Unit 1
- Teacher's DVD-ROM: Unit 1 Test
- Teacher's DVD-ROM Test Generator: Unit 1

2

On the Farm!

Target language

Reading skills:	reading for gist / specific information (matching headings to paragraphs, comprehension questions)
Vocabulary:	topic vocabulary (farm life), general basic vocabulary (time)
Grammar:	present simple, adverbs of frequency
Listening skills:	listening for gist / specific information (multiple matching, multiple choice)
Speaking skills:	talking about daily activities
Pronunciation skills:	tongue twister with *s* and *sh*
Writing skills:	informal email (1)

Get ready!

Aim: to learn the names of young animals

- Ask students if they have pets at home. Can they see an animal that looks like their pet in the pictures?
- Select a student to read the animal names.
- Explain these are the names for the young of each animal.
- Give students a short time to match the names to the pictures.
- You may wish to refer students to the *Vocabulary database* on page 139.
- Review answers orally.

1 d	3 b	5 g	7 e
2 c	4 a	6 f	

Reading

Aim: to give practice in reading for gist and specific information about farm life

Warm up!

Aim: to familiarise students with names for animals and their young

- Ask students to tell the class what their favourite farm animal is and why, eg *I like ducks because they walk funny. I like dogs because they are our friends.*
- Ask the class to say what we call the animal's baby, eg *dog/puppy, cow/calf, duck/duckling,* etc.

1

- Pick a volunteer to read the first paragraph of the advert aloud.
- Ask students to say what might be a good heading for the first paragraph. Explain that a heading gives the gist of a paragraph in just a few words.
- Pick volunteers to read each of the remaining paragraphs aloud.
- Give students a short time to match each paragraph with the headings.
- Review answers orally.

1 b	3 d	5 e
2 f	4 a	6 c

2

- Ask students to think about the different people and animals mentioned in the advert. Who did they learn about by name? Which others were mentioned?
- Ask students to read the advert again, to themselves this time.
- Give them a short time to complete the table.
- Check answers orally and/or by writing them on the board.

Types of animal	Types of people	Names of people and animals
cat dog hamster farm animal(s) cow(s) chicken(s) horse(s) sheep sheepdog duck(s) goat(s) baby animal(s) chick(s) duckling(s) calf (calves) pony (ponies) lamb puppy (puppies) kitten(s) donkey	*the public* farm worker(s) parent(s) child(ren) teacher(s) student(s) young child(ren) older child(ren) visitor(s)	*Mr and Mrs Collins* Sally (the sheepdog) Ned (the old donkey)

3

- Give students a short time to answer the questions using a word or short phrase.
- Invite them to refer back to the advert if necessary.
- Review answers orally.

1 in a town or a city (Do you live in a town or a city? These days, most people do.)
2 seven/7 (it's open to the public seven days a week,…)
3 5.30am (Farm life starts early (at 5.30am!))
4 six/6 o'clock / 6am (People start arriving at six o'clock.)
5 seven/7 in the evening / seven/7 o'clock / 7pm (…and leave at seven in the evening.)
6 (a lovely) lunch (We have a lovely lunch at one o'clock,…)
7 tea and cake (…and tea and cake in the afternoon.)
8 on the duckpond (Young children love feeding the ducks on the duckpond.)

4

- Share an example of something you'd like to do at *Amberton Farm*, eg *I'd like to brush the horses.*
- Check that students understand how and when to use the structure *would like to do*… .
- Ask students to think of what they'd like to do; give them a short time to write their answer.
- Invite students to read their sentences aloud.

Cool down!

Aim: to give practice naming animal types and animal names

- Write the following sentence on the board:

ON THE BOARD

I have a pet pig. Her name is Pickles.

- Ask students to use their imagination and think of a creative name for an unusual pet; refer to the example on the board.
- Invite them to have fun naming their own unusual pet by completing the sentence: *I have a pet* ________. *His/Her name is* ________.

Wordpower!

Aim: to develop students' topic vocabulary

- Tell students that all the answers appear in the advert they have read.
- Ask students to try to fill in the gaps without referring back to the text, but explain they can if necessary.
- You may wish to refer students to the *Vocabulary database* on page 139.
- Remind students they should write only one letter in each gap, and the first letter has been given to help them.
- Check answers orally and/or by writing them on the board.

1 welcome	4 move	7 touch
2 feed	5 plant	8 stroke
3 collect	6 pick	

Additional Task

- Mime an animal and ask *What am I?*
- Ask students to shout out what animal they think you are, eg *You're a duck!, You're a duckling!*
- You may wish to make this a game where if a student gets it right, they can mime an animal for everyone else.

HOMEWORK!

Assign exercises 1–3 on pages 10 and 11 of the Workbook.

Grammar 1 G

Present simple

Aim: to facilitate students' understanding of the functions and usage of the present simple

Warm up!

Aim: to consider events that always happen at the same time

- Ask students to think about things they always do at certain times of the day, week or year.
- Ask them to take turns telling the class what they always do at certain times of the day, week or year.

- Examples: *I have a birthday party every year. I play football at the weekends. I walk to school every morning. I eat lunch at 12 o'clock.* etc.

Grammar presentation 1

- Go through the grammar presentation with students. Check they understand when we use the present simple (to talk about situations that always or never happen, or happen generally, every day, regularly, usually, often or sometimes).
- Explain to students that there is more information on the present simple in *Grammar database 3* on page 146 at the back of the book.
- Ask them to read through the information in the *Grammar database* on their own.
- Ask them if they have any questions.
- Ask students to complete the Quick check task on page 146.
- Check answers orally and ask students to justify their answers, eg *1 She loves* because with *he/she/it* the verb takes an *-s* or *-es*.

Quick check

Circle these correct answers:
1 loves
2 Do you go
3 don't feed
4 Yes, I do.
5 teaches

1

- Give the students a short time to circle the correct word or phrase to complete each sentence.
- Review answers orally.

1 wake up	3 live	5 like
2 eats	4 go	6 wants

2

- Review the correct way to form a negative with the verb *do*, ie *don't/doesn't*.
- Go over the first sentence together.
- Give students a short time to make the rest of the sentences negative.
- Go round the class helping students where necessary.
- Check answers orally and/or by writing them on the board.

2 This dog doesn't eat chocolate!
3 The ducks don't live on the duckpond.
4 We don't go to the farm every Saturday.
5 I don't like Ned the donkey.
6 She doesn't want to live on a farm.

3

- Review the correct way to form a question from a statement, ie placing *Do/Does* at the beginning of the sentence and removing the *-s* or *-es* from the verb.
- Go over the first sentence together.
- Give students a short time to write the rest of the questions.
- Go round the class helping students where necessary.
- Check answers orally and/or by writing them on the board.

2 Does this dog eat chocolate?
3 Do the ducks live on the duckpond?
4 Do we/you go to the farm every Saturday?
5 Do I/you like Ned the donkey?
6 Does she want to live on a farm?

4

- Students should be able to complete this exercise on their own.
- Give them a short time to put the verbs into the correct form.
- Assign students to read out the paragraphs when they have finished.

1 works	6 does	10 teaches
2 loves	7 feeds	11 visit
3 gets up	8 makes	12 don't stay
4 goes	9 cooks	13 Do you want
5 doesn't come		

Cool down!

Aim: to give extra practice in using the present simple

- Write the following phrases on the board:

ON THE BOARD

make breakfast go to school go to work
stay at home

- Ask students to tell the class who in their family does each of the activities on the board.
- Ask them in pairs to take turns telling each other the answers.

HOMEWORK!

Assign exercises 1–4 on pages 11 and 12 of the Workbook.

Wordpower!

Aim: to develop students' topic vocabulary

1

- Ask students if they know what time the school day begins and ends. If there is a clock in the room, ask them to say what time it is now.
- Check they use correct vocabulary to say the times.
- Remind students there are different ways to say what time it is, eg *five forty-five* is the same as *quarter to six.*
- Give them a short time to label the clocks.
- You may wish to refer students to the *Vocabulary database* on page 139.

- Review answers orally.

1 a second	5 half past three
2 a minute	6 three o'clock
3 an hour	7 quarter to three
4 a watch	

2

- Explain to students that the words in bold are in the wrong sentences.
- Give students time to write the correct words on the lines.
- Assign a student to read out the paragraph when they have finished.

1 watch	4 seconds	7 quarter
2 o'clock	5 half	8 to
3 minutes	6 past	9 hour

HOMEWORK!

Assign exercises 1 and 2 on page 13 of the Workbook.

Listening

Aim: to give practice in listening for gist and specific information

Warm up!

Aim: to introduce the topic of time and schedules

- Write the following phrases on the board:

ON THE BOARD

many times a day   once a day
once a week   once a year

- Divide students into four groups.
- Assign one category from the board to each group.
- Give students a short time to come up with a list of activities they do *many times a day*, *once a day*, *once a week* or *once a year* (depending on their group's category).
- Ask them to choose one person from each group to note down their answers.
- When they have finished, ask the group's note-taker to share the answers by reading the list aloud.

1

- Explain to students they will be listening to five people talking about *Amberton Farm*.
- Ask students to predict what the speakers might talk about based on the advert they read on page 15, eg *What types of animals might they talk about? What types of farm chores might they describe?*
- Ask students to listen for clues about what times of day the chores are performed.
- Ask students to choose the correct answers as they listen.
- Play the CD track once all the way through. Repeat if necessary.
- Review answers orally.

1 e	2 a	3 d	4 b	5 c

CD Track 5

2

- Explain to students they will listen to the recording again.
- Ask students to choose the correct answers as they listen.
- Play the CD track once all the way through. Repeat if necessary.
- Review answers orally.

1 B (…at about five o'clock …)
2 A (…I usually get up at quarter to five!)
3 C (…we usually work seven days a week,…)
4 C (…but I can only go to the farm once a month …)
5 B (I think it's a wonderful place!)

CD Track 5

3

- Ask students to talk about themselves by answering the questions about farm life.
- You may wish to have students share their answers with the class, or you may want to divide them into pairs and share their answers with a partner.
- Go round the class helping students where necessary.

Cool down!

Aim: to encourage students to relate the listening recording to their own experience

- Ask students to say how their lives are similar or different to a farmer's, eg *A farmer gets up early every morning, but I don't get up early every morning. A farmer feeds the chickens, but I feed my puppy.* etc.

HOMEWORK!

Assign exercises 1 and 2 on page 13 of the Workbook.

Speaking

Aim: to give practice in talking about daily activities

Warm up!

Aim: to introduce the topic of daily schedules

- Say to students *We are going to play Timeline.*
- Ask them to note down on a piece of paper their favourite time of day and the activity they do at that time, eg *3:30 - I go to football practice.*

- When they have finished writing, ask them to stand and hold their piece of paper in front of them so everyone can see.
- Give them a short time to arrange themselves one by one to the front of the class in a *Timeline*, positioning themselves in the correct chronological order.
- Don't worry if there are duplicate times; let those students stand together.

1

- Ask students to form pairs and select a role (Student A or Student B) for a small role-play exercise.
- Give them a short time to read through and say the dialogue.

2

- While still in pairs, students should quietly read through the list and fill in their own answers in the first column.
- You may wish to encourage them to add one additional question which is not on the list.

3

- Explain that the student pairs should interview each other to complete the second column.
- Explain to them that they may use the dialogue from exercise 1 as a reference.
- If they added the additional question in column 1, encourage them to ask that question too in order to complete the exercise.
- Go round the class helping students where necessary.

4

- Go through the *Phrase Bank!* with students before asking them to do exercise 4.
- Point out that we use these words and phrases to talk about time.
- You may wish to refer students to the *Speaking database* on page 143.
- Call upon each pair of students to stand and present their answers to the class.
- Ask each student in the pair to tell the class about his/her friend, using their notes from the second column.

Cool down!

Aim: to give students additional practice in talking about daily activities

- Explain to students that this time they will present their own answers from the first column to the class.
- Call upon students to stand and tell the class what their daily activities are.

SoundSpot

Aim: to give practice in saying phrases with multiple similar sounds

1

- Explain that a sentence or phrase with many similar sounds that make it difficult to pronounce is called a 'tongue twister'.
- Ask students to say the sentence in exercise 1 very slowly.

2

- Ask students to listen closely to the recording and repeat the sentence.
- Play the CD track once all the way through. Repeat if necessary.

CD Track 7

3

- Explain that tongue twisters can be fun when you try to say them fast.
- Ask students to say the sentence in exercise 1 as fast as they can.
- Tell them to have fun with it and not worry when their tongues become twisted. That's what makes it fun!

Additional Task

- Write the following sentence on the board:

ON THE BOARD

I'm sure she sells sea shells.

- Say to students *We're going to have more fun with tongue twisters.*
- Read – or ask a brave volunteer to read – the tongue twister on the board.
- Get students to take turns repeating it as quickly as possible.

Grammar 2 G

Adverbs of frequency

Aim: to introduce the use of adverbs to describe frequency

Warm up!

Aim: to consider events that occur often, sometimes or never

- Ask students *How often do you clean your room?* and write the following words on the board:

ON THE BOARD

often   sometimes   never

- Ask students to think about their chores and activities.
- Ask them to use one of the words on the board in a sentence that answers the question *How often do you clean your room?* eg *I sometimes clean my room.*
- Ask them to take turns telling what other chores or activities they do *often*, *sometimes* or *never*.

Grammar presentation 2

- Go through the grammar presentation with students.
- Explain that we use adverbs of frequency – *never, sometimes, often, usually, always* – to show how frequently something happens.
- Refer students to the information on adverbs of frequency in *Grammar database 4* on page 146 at the back of the book.
- Ask them to read through the information in the *Grammar database* on their own.
- Ask them if they have any questions.
- Ask students to complete the Quick check task on page 147.
- Check answers orally and ask students to justify their answers, eg *1 is often tired.* because adverbs of frequency usually go after the verb *be*.

Quick check

Circle these correct answers:
1 is often tired
2 Are they usually
3 never go to the cinema
4 Do you often
5 I have a haircut every week.

1

- Remind students that certain phrases – *every hour/day/week/year,* etc – go at the end of a sentence.
- Give students a short time to rewrite each sentence so the word or phrase in bold is in the correct place.
- Check answers orally and/or by writing them on the board.

2 Our cat is always ill.
3 My dog usually eats three meals a day.
4 My mum often rides horses.
5 Do you sometimes go to the farm?
6 I never get up at five o'clock in the morning.
7 That duck never flies.
8 Ned has an apple every day.

2

- Review the chart with students and make sure they understand how to use the key.
- Give them a short time to write sentences using the information from the chart.
- Check answers orally and/or by writing them on the board.

2 Ned eats apples every day.
3 Clever never plays with the visitors.
4 Hamish usually makes funny noises.
5 Sally sometimes eats apples.
6 Clever often makes funny noises.
7 Milk is never happy.
8 Hamish plays with the visitors every day.
9 Ned is always happy.

3

- Put students into pairs and have them ask and answer the questions.
- Go round the class helping students where necessary. Ask students to tell you something about themselves that is the same or different from their interview partner.

Cool down!

Aim: to give further practice using adverbs of frequency

- Make up statements about farm animals using adverbs of frequency, and ask students to guess what animal you are.
- Examples: *I give milk every day.* (You are a cow.) *I often lay eggs.* (You are a chicken.) *I often swim in a pond.* (You are a duck.) *I usually eat carrots.* (You are a rabbit.)
- Note that there may be more than one correct answer for each.

HOMEWORK!

Assign exercises 1–4 on pages 14 and 25 of the Workbook.

Writing

Aim: to develop the skills necessary to write an informal email

Warm up!

Aim: to familiarise students with the concept of informal emails

- Write the following words on the board:

ON THE BOARD

who why what

- Ask students to tell you who they would write an email to. (Any answer is acceptable.)
- Ask why they might choose an email to communicate (instead of making a phone call, sending a letter, or talking in person).
- Ask what type of content they would include in the email.

1

- Explain that an email has different parts: *address, subject, greeting, message, signing off, sender.*
- Read the email together (in the order it is shown) and point out some of the different parts.
- Give students a short time to put the parts into the correct order.
- Review answers orally.

1 g	3 c	5 e	7 h
2 f	4 a	6 b	8 d

2

- Ask students to read the email again and complete the sentences.
- Review the answers together orally.

1 C	2 A

Language Lab

Aim: to focus on key language found in an informal email

- Ask students to read the statements aloud.
- Check their understanding of words such as 'surnames'.
- Ask students to find and underline the examples individually, or to work together as a class.

1 Hi, Mark! Paul

2

Every day we get up at half past five and help the farmer milk the cows. Then we feed the other animals. There are lots of animals here – cows, horses, sheep, donkeys, goats, chickens, ducks, dogs, cats!
We have lunch at one o'clock. Then, in the afternoon, we play with the animals or sometimes ride horses.
After we feed the animals, we have breakfast. That's at eight o'clock. Then we do jobs on the farm. I often collect the chickens' eggs and brush the horses.
In the evening, I'm usually tired so I go to bed early – at about nine o'clock!

3

We get up at half past five every day …
… or sometimes ride horses.
I often collect the chickens' eggs …
In the evening, I'm usually tired …

4

We get up at half past five every day and help the farmer milk the cows. Then we feed the other animals.
We have lunch at one o'clock. Then, in the afternoon,…
After we feed the animals, we have breakfast. That's at eight o'clock. Then we do jobs on the farm.

Cool down!

Aim: to personalise what the students have just read

- Ask students if they have ever received an email from a friend or family member.
- Encourage discussion about the kinds of messages the emails contained.

HOMEWORK!

Assign exercises 1 and 2 on page 15 of the Workbook.

Plan your project!

Aim: to guide students through the process of writing an informal email

1

- Explain to students that they're going to write an informal email similar to Paul's.
- Ask them to imagine they are on holiday on a farm.
- Give them a short time to answer the questions, using their imagination to make up the information.
- Explain they will use this information to create the content for their email.

2

- Explain to students that they are going to complete the *Planner*.
- Point to the first column and explain that these are the different parts of an email.
- Point to the second column and explain that this is useful information about each part.
- Ask the students to write as much information as they can (in note form) in the third column.
- Encourage them to use their imagination and the information they noted down in exercise 1.
- Check their planners before moving on to exercise 3.

3

- You may wish to assign this for homework or, if there's time, have the students do it in class.
- Explain to students that they're going to use their notes from the *Planner* in exercise 2 to write their email.
- Explain to them that using their notes is not cheating and that it's important to make a detailed plan before you start writing.
- Invite them to look back at Paul's email to help guide them through the task. At this stage, the most important thing is that the students create a successful piece of writing.
- You may also wish them to consult the *Writing database* on page 134, which has a further model to study.
- You may wish to encourage stronger students to take risks with their writing, but it's probably best if weaker students follow the model completely.
- Encourage the students to add command buttons (write, reply, send) and an email address to their email to make it look more authentic.
- You may wish to comment on the students' writing before they produce a final version.

Additional Tasks and Tests

- Page 156: Units 1–2 Song
- Student's CD-ROM: Unit 2
- Teacher's DVD-ROM: Unit 2 Test
- Teacher's DVD-ROM Test Generator: Unit 2

Units 1-2 Revision

You may wish to use this section in any of the following ways with your class.

As a test

- Advise students a few days in advance that they should review the language from Units 1 and 2.
- Before beginning, go through the instructions for each exercise, making sure students understand what is required of them.
- Give students approximately 30 minutes to complete the exercises in test conditions.
- Collect students' books and mark the tests yourself, handing them back the following lesson. Alternatively, go over the answers in the same lesson and ask students to swap books with their partner and mark each other's work.
- The total number of marks for the test is 47 and the following should be taken as a rough guide to students' performance:

43 and over: Brilliant!
38 to 42: Very good!
34 to 37: Good!
25 to 33: Could be better …
24 or under: Should be better …

As homework

- Assign all of the exercises after Units 1 and 2 have been completed.
- Go through the instructions for each exercise as you assign them, making sure students understand what is required of them.
- You may want to ask students to complete this section without referring back to the units at all.
- Check answers in class orally and/or by writing them on the board.

As classwork

- You may wish to use exercises from this section as supplementary material if you feel that a certain language area needs more work.
- Select the exercises which you feel best suit your students' needs, and assign them either as pair work or to be done alone.

1

1 great-grandmother
2 uncle
3 niece
4 cousin
5 nephew
6 great-grandfather

2

1 lambs
2 puppy
3 collects
4 ducklings
5 kitten
6 feed
7 stroking
8 chicks

3

1 half past
2 minutes
3 quarter to
4 o'clock
5 seconds
6 hours

4

1 am
2 in
3 long
4 have got
5 only
6 have
7 best

5

1 are
2 get up
3 wakes
4 are
5 collects
6 feed
7 Do, have
8 have got
9 don't have
10 come

6

1 B 2 A 3 C 4 B

7

1 I'm sorry. I thought this book was ~~my~~, but it's not. **mine**
2 Do you know ~~Davids'~~ phone number? **David's**
3 The ~~girls~~ bedroom is really untidy! **girls'**
4 I've got my homework. Have you got ~~you~~? **yours**
5 Oh, no! I've got ~~mine~~ brother's schoolbag instead of mine! **my**
6 Jen and Jack have got a CD for ~~they dad~~ birthday. **their dad's**

3

Going Shopping!

Target language

Reading skills: reading for gist / specific information (multiple matching, T/F)
Vocabulary: topic vocabulary (shopping), general basic vocabulary (size and shape)
Grammar: present continuous, pronouns
Listening skills: listening for gist / specific information (multiple choice – pictures, sentence completion)
Speaking skills: talking about what people are doing at the moment
Pronunciation skills: pronunciation of similar sounding words
Writing skills: description of a picture of people

Get ready!

Aim: to learn and use phrases to talk about shopping

- Ask students to look at the pictures and say what these items are, eg toy cars, a book, meat, clothes, flowers, CDs, shoes, fruit and vegetables.
- Ask students to say which of these things they often buy, eg *I often buy clothes and CDs.* Then ask students to say which of these things they never buy, eg *I never buy meat or flowers.*
- Give students a short time to match each word or phrase with a picture.
- You may wish to refer students to the *Vocabulary database* on page 139.
- Check answers orally or write the numbers of the pictures on the board along with the correct word or phrase.

1 toy shop	5 florist's
2 bookshop	6 music shop
3 butcher's	7 shoe shop
4 clothes shop	8 grocer's

Reading

Aim: to give practice in reading for gist and specific information

Warm up!

Aim: to give further practice in talking about shopping

- Write the following words on the board:

ON THE BOARD

PERSON	WHAT THEY LIKE
mum	books
dad	music
brother	toys
friend	clothes

- Using the first person in the list as an example, make one or two sentences to talk about what that person likes and where they buy those items from, eg *My mum likes books. She buys books at the bookshop.*
- Ask a student to make sentences using the second person. If that student gets it right, they can ask another student to make sentences with the third person.
- If time permits, you can come up with more people and things to buy, or ask students to come up with more examples using the items from the *Get ready!* task or any other items they can think of.

1

- Ask students to silently and individually read the dialogue. Encourage them to ignore all unknown vocabulary at this stage.
- Ask students some very general and simple questions about the text, eg *What kind of text is it?* (a dialogue), *Who are the speakers?* (Grace and Lily), *What is the dialogue about?* (shopping)
- Give students a couple of minutes to do exercise 1.
- Review answers orally.

1 L   2 G   3 L   4 G

2

- Encourage students to do this task quickly but carefully (to help develop their scanning skills).

- Explain to students that they should decide whether each statement is true or false and circle 'T' or 'F' next to each statement.
- Encourage students to underline in the text where they find the answer.
- When they have finished, discuss the answers together. Encourage students to justify their answers by giving reasons.

> 1 F (I'm getting some good ideas for my dad's birthday next week.)
> 2 T (The shopping centre's busy, isn't it?)
> 3 F (Everything is so expensive, though, and I don't have a lot of money.)
> 4 F (The ones I have are fine, but they don't match my skirt for the party.)
> 5 F (I'm looking for some new socks…)
> 6 F (Grace: They're having a sale in that clothes shop! Let's go and see!
> Lily: OK. But then *Chicken World*!)

3

- Use the questions in this task as an oral exercise with as many students as time permits.
- Alternatively, you can write the reasons students like or don't like shopping on the board in two columns.

Cool down!

Aim: to encourage students to talk about what they do when they go shopping

- Ask students to say what they do when they are in a shopping centre, eg *I like to look around, but I don't buy a lot of things.*
- Ask students to compare their shopping trips to Grace and Lily's. Encourage them to say what they do that's similar, eg *I get good ideas for birthdays like Lily does,* and different, eg *Grace likes shopping, but I don't.*

Wordpower!

Aim: to develop students' topic vocabulary

- Tell students that all the answers appear in the dialogue they have read.
- Ask students to try to complete the gaps without referring back to the text, but explain that they can if necessary.
- Remind students that they should only write one letter in each gap and that the first letter has been given to help them.
- Encourage them to be careful with their spelling.
- You may wish to refer students to the *Vocabulary database* on page 139.
- Check the answers orally by asking students to read out the sentences.

1 enjoy	4 expensive	7 lift
2 busy	5 cheap	8 escalator
3 Customers	6 Getting	

HOMEWORK!

Assign exercises 1–4 on pages 17 and 18 of the Workbook.

Grammar 1

Present continuous

Aim: to facilitate students' understanding of the functions and usage of the present continuous

Warm up!

Aim: to practise talking about things that are happening now or around now

- Write the following words on the board:

ON THE BOARD

WE ARE...

sit	English
learn	grammar
look at	in class
talk about	our books

- Ask students to match the verbs on the left with the words and phrases on the right, eg *Sit* goes with *in class.* Explain that some of the verbs can go with more than one of the words or phrases.
- Ask students to make sentences using the present continuous, eg *We are sitting in class. We are learning English. We are learning grammar. We are talking about English. We are looking at our books.* etc.

Grammar presentation 1

- Go through the grammar presentation with students. Check they understand when we use the present continuous (to talk about things happening now or around now).
- Explain to students that there is more information on the present continuous in *Grammar database 5* on page 147 at the back of the book.
- Ask them to read through the information in the *Grammar database* on their own.
- Ask them if they have any questions.
- Ask students to complete the Quick check task on page 147.
- Check answers orally and ask students to justify their answers, eg 1 *Tim's doing his homework.* because we form the present continuous with the correct form of the *be* verb and the *-ing* form of the main verb.

> **Quick check**
>
> Circle the following words and phrases:
> 1 Tim's doing
> 2 Yes, I am.
> 3 are you doing
> 4 Are
> 5 it's raining

1

- Explain to students that they will look at each of the sentences and tick the correct ones, underline the mistakes in the incorrect ones and write the correct word or words.
- Check answers orally and/or by writing them on the board.

1 ✓
2 Do you having fun, or shall we go home? (Are)
3 Jim not buying anything – he's only looking. (Jim is/Jim's)
4 Are the boys wait for us outside the shopping centre? (waiting)
5 My mum's is shopping and Dad's cooking dinner. (mum is/mum's)
6 People not are spending a lot of money on clothes these days. (are not/aren't)
7 ✓
8 Let's hurry up! The shop closing now. (shop is closing/shop's closing)

2

- Explain to students that all these sentences take the present continuous form of the verbs in bold.
- Ask students to write the appropriate negative and question forms of the present continuous where necessary.
- Check answers orally and/or by writing them on the board.

1 am having/'m having
2 are building/'re building
3 are not listening/'re not listening/aren't listening
4 Are you looking
5 is paying/'s paying
6 are wasting/'re wasting
7 am talking/'m talking
8 Is he getting

3

- Ask students to look at the picture and say what the boy is doing, eg *He's holding a phone. He's talking on the phone. He's listening to a friend. He's standing in a shop. He's wearing a shirt.* Then ask students to complete the text with the verbs given.
- When students have finished, check their answers together. Ask a student to read the text aloud.

1 am waiting/'m waiting
2 are standing/'re standing
3 am coming/'m coming
4 am taking/'m taking
5 am turning/'m turning
6 am walking/'m walking
7 am going/'m going
8 am turning/'m turning
9 Are, wearing
10 are waving/'re waving

Cool down!

Aim: to review the functions and usage of the present continuous

- Ask students to pretend it's 6pm and they're at home. Ask a student to say what they're doing right now, eg *I'm doing my homework. I'm watching TV. I'm eating a snack.* etc.
- Encourage them to make statements using the negative form, eg *I'm not playing computer games. I'm reading a book.* Alternatively, you can ask students to form pairs and ask and answer questions in the present continuous form while pretending it's 6pm, eg *Are you eating dinner now? No, I'm watching TV.* etc.

HOMEWORK!

Assign exercises 1–4 on pages 19 and 20 of the Workbook.

Wordpower!

Aim: to develop students' ability to recognise and use words describing size and shape

1

- Ask students to look at the words given and place them in the left column of the table if they describe shape and in the right column of the table if they describe size.
- Encourage students to make a guess if they're not sure.
- You may also wish to refer students to the *Vocabulary database* on page 139.
- Play the recording and check answers together with the students.

Words to describe shape	Words to describe size
circular	*small*
flat	little
narrow	tiny
rectangular	*big*
round	gigantic
square	huge
thick	large
thin	
triangular	
wide	

CD Track 7

Additional Task

- Go round the classroom and ask students to describe different objects in the room using the words from exercise 1, eg *This desk is big, wide and rectangular. This clock is small and round. This book is thick. This pencil is round and thin.* etc.

2

- Ask students to form pairs, look at the pictures and choose one of them to describe to their partner. Alternatively, they can describe any other object they can think of, eg *This is round and red. We eat it.* (a tomato or an apple) When the partner guesses the right object, they should swap roles.
- You can also play this as a game with all the students. Ask one student to describe an object, and when another student guesses correctly, that student can describe another object.

HOMEWORK!

Assign exercises 1 and 2 on page 20 of the Workbook.

Listening

Aim: to give practice in listening for gist and specific information

Warm up!

Aim: to practise listening to conversations

- Ask students to look at the pictures.
- Ask simple questions about the pictures and elicit responses, eg *What are the pictures in each of these groups?* (clothes, fruit and vegetables, books), *Where can people get these things?* (clothes shop, grocer's, book shop)

1

- Explain to students that they are going to listen to three conversations.
- Ask students to predict what the conversations might be about, eg *These people are shopping for these items.*
- Ask students to choose the correct answer, A, B or C, for each conversation.
- Play the CD track once all the way through. Repeat if necessary.

1 B (We're having a sale on T-shirts and jeans at the moment, so it's half price.
Customer: Oh. OK. Yes, this is perfect.)
2 A (We've got Italian tomatoes over here. … Shall I put some in a bag for you?
Customer: Yes, please.)
3 B (*Sun at Night*. What's it about? … Well, that's just the kind of book I like. … I'll just take this book, then.)

CD Track 8

2

- Explain to students that they will listen to the recording again.
- Ask them to read through the sentences before they listen, and to predict the answers.
- Play the CD track again. Pause when you hear the first correct answer (*her birthday*), and ask students to complete the gap. Check their answers.
- Play the rest of the recording in its entirety and ask students to listen and work independently to complete the rest of the gaps.
- Check answers together with students. If necessary, play the recording again for students to check incorrect answers.

1 her birthday (It's her birthday next week…)
2 expensive (It's expensive, though.)
3 good (They cost more than the others, but they're very good.)
4 the supermarket (next door) (Try the supermarket next door.)
5 love story (It's a love story.)
6 two brothers (It's an exciting story about two brothers.)

CD Track 8

3

- Ask students to form pairs and ask and answer the questions from the exercise. When one of the students has asked all the questions, they should swap roles.
- Go round the class helping students where necessary.

Cool down!

Aim: to personalise what the students have listened to

- Ask students about the books in conversation 3. Ask them to talk about which ones they like or don't like and why, eg *I like* The Second Man *because I like stories about families. I don't like* Sun at Night *because I don't like love stories.* etc.

HOMEWORK!

Assign exercises 1 and 2 on page 20 of the Workbook.

Speaking

Aim: to provide practice in talking about what people are doing at the moment

Warm up!

Aim: to develop ideas for talking about what people are doing at the moment

- Go round the class. Ask students to think of people they know that are not in the classroom, eg *my mum, my dad, my friend Katie, my sister, my brother, my science teacher, my doctor, my neighbour,* etc. Write all the people on the board.
- Encourage students to come up with as many people as they can.

1

- Ask students to use different people on the board from the *Warm up!* exercise and say where they think each one is right now.
- When they have finished, check the answers orally, or write their answers on the board next to the appropriate people.

2

- Go through the *Phrase Bank!* with students before you ask students to do exercise 2.
- Put students into pairs, or allow them to choose their own partner.
- Explain that they're going to say what they think the people they chose for exercise 1 are doing right now.
- Ask one student in each pair to talk about each person from exercise 1.
- When that student has talked about each person, they should swap roles.
- You may also wish to refer students to the *Speaking database* on page 143.
- Go round the class helping students where necessary.

3

- With the students still in pairs, ask them to look at the clock and imagine it's that time of the day, and to repeat exercise 2 accordingly.
- You can make it a game by asking one student to choose the time of the day that the other student, or all the students, must talk about.

Cool down!

Aim: to give students additional practice with talking about what people are doing

- Invite students to name some famous people they know and write the names on the board.
- Ask students to talk about what they think the famous people are doing right now.

SoundSpot

Aim: to give practice in pronouncing similar sounding words

1

- Ask students to look at the four words and tick which two words sound the same.
- Encourage them to say the words aloud, but don't correct their pronunciation or answers at this stage.
- Play the recording and then check students' answers.
- Point out that many words in English sound the same but have different spellings.

we're where ✓ were wear ✓

CD Track 9

2

- Explain to students that they are going to listen to a recording of the two sentences in the book. Ask students to say each sentence aloud.
- Play the recording, and ask students to repeat the sentences as they hear them.
- Remind them to be careful of the pronunciations of *we're, wearing, where* and *were.*

CD Track 10

Additional Task

- Write the following words on the board:

ON THE BOARD

here	her	hear
two	too	toe
met	meat	meet
buy	bye	by

- Ask students to look at the words and say which word from each group sounds different from the other two (*her, toe, met*). Note that in the last group of words, all the words sound the same. See if students can discover that they all sound the same without your help.

Grammar 2

Pronouns
Aim: to facilitate students' understanding of the functions and usage of pronouns

Warm up!

Aim: to consider the form of subject, object and reflexive pronouns

- Write on the board:

ON THE BOARD

I	______	myself
______	you	yourself
he	him	______
she	______	herself
it	it	______
we	______	ourselves
they	them	______

- Ask students to look at the words on the board and decide which words are missing (*me, you, himself, her, itself, us, themselves*).

Grammar presentation 2

- Go through the grammar presentation with students. Check they understand when we use each of the pronouns in the presentation.

- Explain to students that there is more information in *Grammar database 6* on page 147 at the back of the book.
- Ask them to read through the information in the *Grammar database* on their own.
- Ask them if they have any questions.
- Ask students to complete the Quick check task on page 147.
- Check answers orally and ask students to justify their answers, eg *1 Give it to her.* because we use the object pronoun when we're talking about who we're giving things to.

Quick check

Circle these correct answers:
1 her
2 itself
3 These
4 that
5 ourselves

1

- Ask students to read the sentences and choose the correct answer, A, B or C.
- When students have finished, check the answers together orally.

1 A	3 A	5 C
2 A	4 B	6 A

2

- Ask students to complete the exercise by using the pronoun in bold and changing it to the correct form to complete the gap.
- When students have finished, check the answers together orally.

1 me	4 himself	7 that
2 yourself	5 her	8 itself
3 these	6 herself	

3

- Ask students to complete the dialogue by putting one word from the box in each gap.
- When students have finished, check the answers together.
- Assign students to read out the dialogue. Time permitting, repeat with as many students as possible.

1 me	4 those	6 myself
2 I	5 you	7 this
3 yourself		

Cool down!

Aim: to review the functions and use of pronouns

- Ask students to look at the picture and think of a sentence without using pronouns, eg *The shop owner is giving a paintbrush to the painter.* Then ask students to replace one or more of the nouns with a pronoun, eg *The shop owner is giving a paintbrush to him. He's giving it to him.* etc.
- Alternatively, you can play a game where you give something to a student and the other students have to use pronouns to describe the action, eg *The teacher is giving the book to Clara. She's giving it to Clara. She's giving it to her.* etc.

HOMEWORK!

Assign exercises 1–4 on pages 21 and 22 of the Workbook.

Writing

Aim: to develop the skills necessary to produce a description of a picture of people

Warm up!

Aim: to familiarise students with the concept of descriptions

- Ask students if they have looked in a magazine that advertises clothes and read a description of what someone is wearing.
- Ask students what kind of information should be in these descriptions.
- Accept all suggestions at this point, but allow students to disagree with each other if they want to.

1

- Ask students to look at the picture and describe a few things that are happening.
- Make notes on the board, or ask students to make notes on a piece of paper.
- With classes of weaker students, you may wish to initially do this as a whole class activity, with students calling out ideas and you writing them on the board, and then have individual students use the information on the board to describe different aspects of the picture.

2

- Ask students to read the description.
- Give them a short time to identify whether the statements are true (T) or false (F).
- Encourage them to underline in the text where they found their answers.
- Check answers together when students have finished.

1 F (It's snowing outside ... I think it's a cold day.)
2 F (I think she's angry because he's sneezing a lot.)
3 T (I think he's trying to catch him and stop him.)
4 F (The baby's wearing pink, so I think it's a girl.)

3

- Ask students to read the description again and match each paragraph with a statement.
- Remind students that one of the statements is used twice.

- Check answers together when students have finished.

1 c	2 b	3 b	4 a

Language Lab

Aim: to focus on key language skills required to achieve this kind of writing task

- Ask students to read the statements aloud.
- Check their understanding of words such as 'opinion' before they attempt the task.
- You may wish students to find and underline the examples individually, or to work together as a class.

1. It's snowing outside, and people are wearing winter clothes. ...two boys are throwing snowballs... They're having a lot of fun! Next to them, a man is sneezing. His wife is looking at him. ...he's sneezing a lot... ...a boy is riding a skateboard. A man is running after him. ...he's trying to catch him... The baby's wearing pink... She's throwing her toys on the floor. Everyone's going in and out of the shops. They're buying things... ...most people are enjoying themselves
2. I think it's a cold day. I think he's got a cold! I think she's angry... I think he's trying to catch him... ...I think it's a girl
3. Near the door... Next to them... In the middle of the shopping centre... In front of them
4. It looks very dangerous! It looks like...

Cool down!

Aim: to personalise what the students have just read

- Ask students to pretend they are at a place in their neighbourhood, eg a restaurant. Ask them to describe the scene.
- Encourage them to use the present continuous in their descriptions, eg *People are eating pizza and enjoying their food. People are talking and laughing. The waiter is bringing food to people's tables.* etc.

HOMEWORK!

Assign exercises 1 and 2 on page 22 of the Workbook.

Plan your project!

Aim: to guide students through the writing process

1

- Explain to students that they are going to write a description similar to the one in the writing section.
- Ask students to look at the picture and explain that the picture is similar to the one they saw in the writing section, but there are some differences.
- Ask the students to describe a few things that are happening in the photo. If you like, you can write their answers on the board or ask them to write them on a separate piece of paper.

2

- Ask students to read the questions and look at the picture again to find the answers.
- Check answers together when students have finished.

3

- Explain to students that they are going to complete the *Planner*.
- Point to the first column and explain that these are the different parts of the description.
- Point to the second column and explain that this is useful information about each part.
- Ask the students to complete the gaps in the third column using the picture and the information they found in exercise 2.
- Check their planners before moving on to exercise 4.

4

- You may wish to assign this for homework or, if there's time, for the students to do this in class.
- Explain to students that they are going to use their notes from the *Planner* in exercise 3 to write their description.
- Explain to them that using their notes is not cheating and that it is important to make a detailed plan before you start writing.
- Allow them to look back at the description in the writing section if they're not sure what to do. At this stage, the most important thing is that the students create a successful piece of writing.
- You may also wish them to consult the *Writing database* on page 134, which has a further model to study.
- You may wish to encourage stronger students to take risks with their writing, but it's probably best if weaker students follow the model completely.
- You may wish to comment on the students' writing before they produce a final version.

Additional Tasks and Tests

- Student's CD-ROM: Unit 3
- Teacher's DVD-ROM: Unit 3 Test
- Teacher's DVD-ROM Test Generator: Unit 3

4

Read All About It!

Target language

Reading skills: reading for gist / specific information (T/F, match questions and answers)
Vocabulary: topic vocabulary (media), ways of talking
Grammar: question words, *too* and *very*
Listening skills: listening for gist / specific information (multiple choice, sentence completion)
Speaking skills: asking and answering questions (1)
Pronunciation skills: pronunciation of question words
Writing skills: interview (dialogue) (1)

Get ready!

Aim: to learn and use words for different types of writings and publications

- Ask students to look at the pictures and say what they are (newspaper, magazines).
- Explain that there are many types of publications where we find news and information; some are printed, some are online and some are both.
- Invite students to talk about where they like to find news and information.
- Give them a short time to tick the words they know and cross the ones they don't.
- You may wish to refer students to the *Vocabulary database* on page 139.
- Review all the words on the list together as a class.

Reading

Aim: to introduce the concept of a pupil website

Warm up!

Aim: to consider news topics that interest students

- Ask students to form two groups and ask *What topics would you like to see on a school website?*
- Ask each group to elect an 'editor'. Each editor will lead the discussion with his/her group and note down the group's ideas.
- Give the groups a short time to discuss which topics would make good pupil website content.
- Bring the two groups together to share their ideas.
- Talk about the similarities and differences between the two groups' ideas.

1

- Choose a few volunteers to read each section of the website aloud.
- Give students a short time to identify whether the statements are true (T) or false (F).
- Review the answers together orally. Encourage students to justify their answers.

1 T (Welcome to the new website for all pupils at Linton School!)
2 F (Three other pupils are helping me:...)
3 F (No teachers work on the site,...)
4 T (Reviews of school plays and concerts... ...we also have articles that we write,... Please email us your articles, short stories or poems.)
5 F (Click here for a special interview with Mr Jennings, the Head!)

2

- Explain to students that all the answers appear in the website they have read.
- Ask students to try to match each question with an answer without referring back to the text, but explain that they can if they need to.
- Check the answers together orally.

1 c (Three other pupils are helping me: Tony Warner, Tariq Sims and Paula Carter.)
2 e (No teachers work on the site,...)
3 a (Reviews of school plays and concerts are in the 'Interesting articles and reviews' section.)
4 b (But we need you to write for us too!)
5 f
6 d (How old are you? ... How many children do you have? ... Who is your favourite actor?, etc.)

3

- Ask students to look at the words in the box.
- If they need help understanding any of the words, encourage them to refer to the *Vocabulary database* on page 139.
- Ask them to complete each sentence with one word from the box.
- Encourage students to make a guess if they're not sure.
- Check the answers orally and/or write answers on the board.

1 website	6 sections
2 newspaper	7 Calendar
3 links	8 poem
4 welcome	9 interview
5 editor	

4

- Ask students *What parts of the pupil website are the same as your group's ideas?*
- Give them a short time to write down what they like about the website.
- Ask students to share their answers with the class.

Cool down!

Aim: to begin thinking like a website reporter

- Ask students to imagine they are website reporters.
- Invite them to think about which section of their pupil website they would like to write articles for, eg sports, play reviews, school news, etc.

Additional task

- Ask students to think of some words that rhyme (eg *book* and *look*).
- Write them on the board.
- Ask students to write a short poem using some or all of the words on the board.

Wordpower!

Aim: to develop students' topic vocabulary

- Tell students that all the answers are in the website content they have read.
- Ask students to try to complete the gaps without referring back to the text, but explain that they can if necessary.
- Remind students they should only write one letter in each gap and that the first letter has been given to help them.
- Remind them to be careful with their spelling.
- You may wish to refer students to the *Vocabulary database* on page 139.
- Check the answers together orally.

1 editor	4 opinion, view
2 reporter	5 programme
3 calendar	6 review

Additional Task

- Say to students *Let's play Web Whispers!*
- Select a player to begin the game by whispering something they read on a school website to the second player.
- The second player will whisper the message to the next player, and so on until everyone has heard/shared the message.
- The last player announces the message to the entire group, and the first student says whether it is the same message that started the game.
- Talk about how different – and amusing – a message can become after it's been passed around many times to different people.

HOMEWORK!

Assign exercises 1–4 on pages 23 and 24 of the Workbook.

Grammar 1 G

Question words

Aim: to facilitate students' understanding of the functions and usage of the words *who, where, what, which, when, why* and *how* to ask questions

Warm up!

Aim: to give practice using *who* and *what* to ask basic questions

- Tell students they are going to play a guessing game.
- Explain that they will take turns briefly describing a person or thing, and then ask either *What am I?* or *Who am I?*
- Start off by describing a student and then an object as examples, eg *I have long brown hair. I am wearing a red shirt. Who am I?* (Maria) *I have four legs. People sit on me. What am I?* (a chair)
- Point out that the word *who* is used to describe people, while the word *what* is used to describe things.

Grammar presentation 1

- Go through the grammar presentation with students.
- Review the uses of each question word and what types of questions are asked with each.
- Explain that we use question words to ask questions that do not have a *yes/no* answer.
- Explain we use the question form of the verb after question words.
- Explain that there is more information on question words in *Grammar database 7* on page 148 at the back of the book.
- Ask students to read through the information in the *Grammar database* on their own.

- Ask them if they have any questions.
- Assign students the Quick check task on page 148.
- Check answers together orally. Point out that item 4 is tricky because both options can work grammatically, but there is only one correct answer. The clue to the correct answer can be found by looking at the question's answer.

Quick check

Circle these correct answers:
1 What time do you
2 are you
3 Who is your favourite singer?
4 When
5 Why

1

- Remind students that question words let you know what type of question is being asked, eg *Who* refers to people, *What* refers to things, *When* refers to time, and so on.
- Encourage them to pay close attention to the question word at the beginning of each interview question as they complete the exercise.
- Give students a short time to match the questions with the correct answers.
- Review the answers together orally and ask students to justify their answers.

1 d	3 b	5 j	7 g	9 i
2 h	4 f	6 a	8 c	10 e

2

- Ask students to choose the correct question word to fill in each gap.
- When students have finished, check the answers together orally.

1 B	3 B	5 B	7 C	9 C
2 A	4 A	6 C	8 B	10 B

Cool down!

Aim: to personalise the exercise and give additional practice with question words

- Ask students by a show of hands to indicate whether they prefer to go to the cinema or to a live sporting event.
- Invite students to answer the following questions: *Why do you prefer this activity? Who is your favourite movie star? Who is your favourite athlete? How often do you go to the cinema? How often do you go to sporting events?*
- If any students indicate they do not attend either type of activity, ask them *What is your favourite past time? How often do you do it?*

HOMEWORK!

Assign exercises 1–4 on pages 24 and 25 of the Workbook.

Wordpower!

Aim: to develop students' topic vocabulary

1

- Say to students *I'm not a teacher; I'm an astronaut.* Say that this is an example of a lie.
- Give examples of a shout, a scream and a whisper. Explain that we can detect certain things about the speaker based on the speaker's use of his/her voice, eg a *whisper* is used to tell a secret or to communicate quietly, a *scream* is used to show excitement, fear or anger.
- Give students a short time to fill in the gaps to complete the definitions.
- You may wish to refer students to the *Vocabulary database* on page 139.
- Review answers together orally.

1 say	6 speak, talk (in either order)
2 whisper	7 speak
3 shout	8 lie
4 scream	9 tell, tell
5 talk	10 tell

2

- Explain to students they will listen to a recording of different phrases and voice styles.
- Ask students to choose the correct answers as they listen.
- Review answers orally together.

1 tell the time	5 speak French
2 whisper	6 talk about the weather
3 scream	7 tell a lie
4 shout	8 tell the truth

CD Track 11

HOMEWORK!

Assign exercises 1 and 2 on page 26 of the Workbook.

Listening

Aim: to give practice in listening for gist and specific information

Warm up!

Aim: to develop skills in listening for clues

- Divide the class into small groups of 3–4 students.
- Ask the groups to quietly plan a school event. They should decide what the event is, when and where the event takes place and who will attend.
- Give them a short time to sort out the details.

- Walk round the room and listen in on the groups as they plan their events. If they have difficulty thinking of an event to plan, you might make suggestions, eg party, picnic, concert, camping trip, play, etc.
- When they are done, play the role of 'reporter' and find out information about their events by asking *who, what, when* and *where* questions.

1

- Explain to students they will be listening to people who have gathered for a meeting.
- Point out that they will only listen to the beginning of the meeting.
- Encourage students to listen for clues to help them determine what the meeting is about.
- Ask students to choose the correct answers as they listen.
- Review answers orally together.

1 C   2 B

CD Track 12

2

- Explain to students they will now listen to the meeting all the way through.
- Ask them to read through the sentences before they listen.
- Ask students to complete the sentences with a word or short phrase.
- Check answers together with students. If necessary, play the recording again for students to check incorrect answers.

2 interview (And I love the interview with Mr Jennings.)
3 30/thirty (…he looks about thirty if you ask me!)
4 Mrs Jennings (OK, so Tariq – you talk to Mrs Jennings)
5 Friday (It's on Friday.)
6 8.30 / eight thirty / half past eight (At eight thirty.)
7 review (…I can write the review.)
8 writing a book (He's writing a book at the moment.)
9 (some) questions (…I'll speak to him in the lunch break and ask him some questions.)

CD Track 12

3

- Ask students to form pairs and ask and answer the questions. When one of the students has asked all the questions, they should swap roles.
- Go round the class helping students where necessary.

Cool down!

Aim: to personalise what the students have listened to

- Ask students to imagine they've been invited to Angela's website meeting.
- Ask them what they would tell Angela they like best about the pupil website.
- Ask them what suggestions they might offer to make the website better.

HOMEWORK!

Assign exercises 1 and 2 on page 26 of the Workbook.

Speaking

Aim: to give practice in asking and answering questions about personal lives

Warm up!

Aim: to introduce basic interview questions and short-answer responses

- Say to students *We're going to play Four or Fewer.*
- Challenge them to answer your interview questions in four words or fewer.
- Explain to students that interview questions can be answered with short phrases. (No need to answer in complete sentences.)
- Go round the room asking each student one of the questions from exercise 1. Ask the questions in random order, not in the order they appear in exercise 1.
- As the students answer, count out the number of words in their answers by holding up your fingers, one finger per word. Stop at four (or fewer). If they continue beyond four words, ask them if there are any words they can cut out and still answer the question.

1

- Put students into pairs, or allow them to choose a partner.
- Explain that they're going to interview each other and provide short answers.
- Give them a short time to fill in the gaps before starting their interviews.
- Remind them to write three questions of their own.

2

- Students should remain in pairs while they individually complete exercise 2. (They will continue their interviews in exercise 3.)
- Give students practice with short answers by completing exercise 2.
- Tell them questions 1–5 can be answered in four words or fewer.
- Give them a short time to cross out the words that are not needed in each answer.
- Review answers together orally.

1 ~~I'm~~ twelve ~~years old~~.
2 ~~My favourite actor is~~ Zac Efron.
3 ~~I get up at~~ half past seven.
4 ~~I live~~ in the town centre.
5 ~~I write poems~~ because it's fun.
6 ~~In my free time, I like~~ playing football and ~~playing~~ computer games.

3

- Invite one student in each pair to begin asking the questions and noting down the other student's replies.
- Remind students to use their questions from exercise 1 (including the three they created on their own).
- Go through the *Phrase Bank!* with students and talk about the style of speaking when asking and answering questions for interviews.
- When one student has asked all the questions, they should swap roles.
- Go round the room and offer help as needed, reminding students to keep their answers short.

Cool down!

Aim: to give students additional practice with interview questions

- Invite students to interview you.
- Let them know you will be answering in complete sentences and it is up to them to shorten your answers.
- Example:
Student: *What do you like doing in your free time?*
Teacher: *I like reading books in my free time.*
Teacher: *What do I like doing in my free time?*
Student: *Reading books.*

SoundSpot

Aim: to give practice in pronouncing words at different tones and volumes

1

- Ask students to listen to the words and repeat them.
- Warn them that they will be said faster each time.
- Encourage them to keep up with the speed, but tell them not to worry if they fall behind.
- Repeat the exercise as necessary. Remind the students to speak as clearly as possible, but have fun with it.

CD Track 14

2

- Ask students to whisper the words in exercise 1 as fast as they can.
- Ask students to say the same words again as fast as they can, this time in a normal tone.
- Ask students to shout the words as fast as they can.
- If there is time, discuss the students' reactions to the exercise. Ask students which words they found most difficult to pronounce. Ask whether the words were more difficult to pronounce while whispering, shouting or speaking in a normal tone.

Grammar 2 G

too* and *very

Aim: to introduce practical uses of *too* and *very*

Warm up!

Aim: to give practice in the use of *too* and *very*

- Write the following words on the board:

ON THE BOARD

This soup is very ________________.
This soup is too ________________.

- Ask students to create sentences by filling in each gap with the same word.
- Explain that the meaning of the sentence changes simply by changing *very* to *too*.

Grammar presentation 2

- Go through the grammar presentation with students. Check they understand the uses of *very* and *too* and the ways they can be used to convey negative or positive meanings.
- Explain that there is more information in *Grammar database 8* on page 148 at the back of the book.
- Ask them to read through the information in the *Grammar database* on their own.
- Ask them if they have any questions.
- Assign students the Quick check task on page 148.
- Check answers together orally.

Quick check

Circle these correct answers:
1 very
2 noisily
3 for you to
4 good
5 very

1

- Ask students to recall which word – *very* or *too* – can be used to express both something positive and negative.
- Give them a short time to select P or N to show whether each sentence is positive or negative.
- Review answers together orally.

1 P	3 P	5 N	7 P
2 N	4 N	6 N	8 N

2

- Encourage students to use their imagination and have fun with this exercise.
- Give them a short time to answer each question using the word *too*.
- Review answers together orally.

Suggested answers:

2 too tired	6 too difficult
3 too expensive	7 too boring
4 too old	8 too hot
5 too big	

3

- Remind students that switching from *very* to *too* can make a positive statement negative.
- Give them a short time to complete the second sentence in each sentence pair.
- Review answers together orally.

> 2 too long (for me) to
> 3 too difficult (for them) to
> 4 too short (for me) to
> 5 too fast (for me) to
> 6 too badly (for me) to
> 7 too slow (for him) to play
> 8 too hot (for me) to

Cool down!

Aim: to give extra practice in the practical uses of *very* and *too*

- Write the following words on the board:

ON THE BOARD

Why do you like ____________?
Because they're very ____________.
Why don't you like ____________?
Because they're too ____________.

- Divide the class into the *Likes* and the *Don't Likes*.
- Ask someone from the *Likes* side of the classroom to tell the class why they like a certain thing, eg cupcakes, skateboards, video games.
- As soon as you get an answer, ask someone from the *Don't Likes* side of the classroom to tell the class why they do not like the same thing.
- Alternate back and forth.

HOMEWORK!

Assign exercises 1–4 on pages 27 and 28 of the Workbook.

Writing

Aim: to develop skills necessary to write an interview

Warm up!

Aim: to familiarise students with questions used in more formal interviews

- Ask students to imagine they are in a lift with their favourite celebrity.
- They will go up four floors in the lift together. What two questions would they ask their favourite celebrity before the doors open and the celebrity gets out?

1

- Ask students to read the interview quietly to themselves.
- Give them a short time to write the correct question words or phrases.
- Review answers together orally.

1	Who	6	How
2	How old	7	What time / When
3	How many	8	Which
4	Where	9	When
5	Why	10	What

2

- Ask students to read the interview again.
- Give them a short time to fill in the gaps.
- Review answers together orally.

> Favourite writer: J.K. Rowling (maybe)
> Age: 36
> Number of children: none/0
> Home: Cornwall
> Reason for living there: (because it's) beautiful and peaceful
> Gets ideas for stories from: (the) news on TV
> Starts writing: 10am/10/ten o'clock
> Number of hours she writes every day: 4 or 5
> Next book in shops: in about 3/three months
> Name of next book: *The Mystery of the Dark Cave*

Language Lab

Aim: to focus on key language and styles found in an interview

- Check students' understanding of terminology such as 'short forms', 'exclamation marks' and 'extra information' before beginning the task.
- You may wish students to find and underline the examples individually, or to work together as a class.

> 1 That's a very difficult question! / Her books are fantastic! / Because it's beautiful and peaceful! / I don't know! / That question's too difficult for me to answer! / I like lots of words! / I don't have a favourite!
> 2 That's a very difficult question! / I'll be 37 next March. / I'm not married.
> I don't know! That question's too difficult for me to answer! / It's called *The Mystery of the Dark Cave*. / I don't have a favourite!
> 3 Maybe J.K. Rowling. / 36. / None. / In Cornwall, in the south-west of England. / Because it's beautiful and peaceful! / At about ten o'clock in the morning.
> 4 Maybe J.K. Rowling. Her books are fantastic! / 36. I'll be 37 next March. /
> None. I'm not married. / In about three months. It's called *The Mystery of the Dark Cave*.

Cool down!

Aim: to give extra practice with short-phrase interview answers

- Say to students *We are going to do a 'backward interview'.*
- Invite students to suggest a random short-phrase answer, and encourage another person to make up a suitable question.
- Examples: (Student 1) *13 years old.* (Student 2) *How old are you?* (Student 1) *Pizza.* (Student 2) *What's your favourite food?*

HOMEWORK!

Assign exercises 1 and 2 on page 28 of the Workbook.

Plan your project!

Aim: to guide students through the process of writing an interview

1

- Explain to students that they're going to write an interview with a famous person for a magazine or website.
- Ask them to think of celebrities they know many facts about, and choose one they'd like to interview.
- Give them a short time to answer the questions, using real information if they know it, or using their imagination to make up the information if they don't.
- Explain they will use this information to begin writing their interview.

2

- Explain to students that they are going to complete the *Planner.*
- Point to the first column and explain that these are question words they can use to prepare their own list of interview questions.
- Point to the second column and explain that this is where they'll note down their short-phrase answers to the interview questions.
- Ask the students to write as much information as they can using complete sentences in the third column.
- Check their planners before moving on to exercise 3.

3

- You may wish to assign this for homework or, if there's time, have the students do it in class.
- Explain to students that they're going to use their notes from the *Planner* in exercise 2 to write their interview.
- Invite them to look back at the Jenny Dawlings interview to help guide them through the exercise.
- You may also wish them to consult the *Writing database* on page 135, which has a further model to study.
- Encourage stronger students to take risks with their writing, but it's probably best if weaker students follow the model completely.
- Encourage students to use magazines or the internet to find pictures of their celebrity to add to their written interview.
- You may wish to comment on the students' writing before they produce a final version.

Additional Tasks and Tests

- Page 156: Units 3–4 Webquest
- Student's CD-ROM: Unit 4
- Teacher's DVD-ROM: Unit 4 Test
- Teacher's DVD-ROM Test Generator: Unit 4

Units 3-4 Revision

You may wish to use this section in any of the following ways with your class:

As a test

- Advise students a few days in advance that they should review the language from Units 3 and 4.
- Before beginning, go through the instructions for each exercise, making sure students understand what is required of them.
- Give students approximately 30 minutes to complete the exercises in test conditions.
- Collect students' books and mark the tests yourself, handing them back the following lesson. Alternatively, go over the answers in the same lesson and ask students to swap books with their partner and mark each other's work.
- The total number of marks for the test is 49 and the following should be taken as a rough guide to students' performance:

44 and over: Brilliant!
40 to 43: Very good!
35 to 39: Good!
26 to 34: Could be better …
25 or under: Should be better …

As homework

- Assign all of the exercises after Units 3 and 4 have been completed.
- Go through the instructions for each exercise when you assign them, making sure students understand what is required of them.
- You may want to ask students to do this section without referring back to the units at all.
- Check answers in class orally, or by writing them on the board.

As classwork

- You may wish to use exercises from this section as supplementary material if you feel that a certain language area needs more work.
- Select the exercises which you feel best suit your students' needs and assign them either as pairwork or to be done alone.

1

1 bookshop
2 busy
3 customer
4 lift
5 expensive
6 clothes shop
7 butcher's
8 florist's

2

1 narrow
2 thin
3 round
4 huge
5 triangular
6 rectangular

3

1 interviews
2 views
3 article
4 email
5 editor
6 newspaper

4

1 I'm listening
2 Are they doing
3 's/is Sarah talking
4 It's not raining/It isn't raining
5 Simon and Greg aren't waiting
6 are we watching

5

1 too
2 very
3 very
4 too
5 too
6 too

6

1 Where
2 When
3 What
4 How
5 Who
6 How
7 Why

7

1 us
2 this
3 those
4 yourself
5 themselves
6 ours

8

1 Who's your favourite actress?
2 Which sport do you prefer watching – tennis or football?
3 What time do you go to bed?
4 Why are you learning English?

5

The Travel Bug!

Target language

Reading skills:	reading for gist / specific information (multiple matching, sentence completion)
Vocabulary:	topic vocabulary (travelling, countries)
Grammar:	past simple – basic irregular verbs, past simple – regular verbs and more irregular verbs
Listening skills:	listening for gist / specific information (multiple matching, sentence completion)
Speaking skills:	talking about travel activities, past events
Pronunciation skills:	stress in names of countries
Writing skills:	blog post (1)

Get ready!

Aim: to learn and use phrases to talk about travelling

- Ask students to look at the title of the unit and to try to guess what it means. (If you have the travel bug, you really enjoy travelling and want to travel all the time. Bug here means illness.)
- Ask students to look at the pictures and ask them which of these modes of transport they have used.
- Ask students some other questions about the photos, eg *Which one of these is fast? Which one is slow? Which one is safe? Which one is dangerous? Which one do you like the best? Which one do you not like at all?* etc.
- Give students a short time to choose the correct word to complete each gap.
- You may wish to refer students to the *Vocabulary database* on page 139.
- Check answers orally and write the numbers of the pictures on the board along with the correct word.

1 plane	3 bus	5 taxi
2 ferry	4 carriage	

Reading

Aim: to give practice in reading for gist and specific information

Warm up!

Aim: to introduce the concept of blogs

- Write these words on the board:

ON THE BOARD

NAME OF BLOG
BLOG INTRODUCTION
TITLE OF BLOG POST
DATE
BLOG POST

- Ask students if they understand what all of the terms on the board are and explain any unknown terms. (A blog is a place on the web where you write things about your life. A blog post is one article in a blog. A title is a name you give to your blog or an article. etc.)
- Then ask students to look at the blog in their Student's Book and find the items for each of these terms. (Name of blog: Rob's Blog, Blog introduction: Hi! I'm Rob! Welcome to my blog…, Title of blog post: Our trip to New York so far!, Date: July 22nd…, Blog post: Wow! New York is fantastic…)

1

- Ask students to silently and individually read the blog. Encourage them to ignore all unknown vocabulary at this stage.
- Ask students some general and simple questions about the blog, eg *Who is the writer?* (Rob), *What is the blog about?* (the writer's trip to New York), *Does the writer seem happy or sad?* (happy)
- Ask students to look at the pictures that show different activities and to match the activities with a place to complete exercise 1. Give them a few minutes to do this. Go round the class helping students where necessary.
- Check answers orally and/or write answers on the board.

1 c	2 b	3 a

2

- Encourage students to do this task quickly but carefully (to help develop their scanning skills).
- Ask students to read the blog post again and write a word or phrase in each gap to complete the sentences.
- When they have finished, discuss the answers together. Encourage students to justify their answers by giving reasons.

1 three days (I can't believe we got here only three days ago!)
2 (a bit) noisy (…so it was easy to find, but it can be a bit noisy.)
3 capital (city) (It's not the capital city of the USA – that's Washington…)
4 a hot dog (I had a hot dog for dinner… It made me feel like I was in America!)
5 expensive (…the ticket for the Observatory is an extra $15. It's expensive,…)
6 photographs (I didn't take any photographs… …but I got some good postcards instead.)
7 had a picnic (…I went in but my parents didn't. They had a picnic…)
8 two horses (After that, we got in a carriage with two horses.)

3

- Ask students to look at the cities in exercise 3 and talk about which city they would like to visit. Ask them to give reasons. Additionally, ask students where each of these cities are.
- Encourage students to talk about what they would like to do in the city they choose, who they would like to go with, when they would like to go, etc.

Cool down!

Aim: to encourage students to talk about their own lives

- Ask students if they've visited a place recently. Ask them some questions about their trip, eg *How did you get there? How long did you stay? Who did you go with? Did you like the food?* etc.
- Ask students to compare their trip to Rob's. Encourage them to say what they did that's similar, eg *I stayed in a hotel too.* and different, eg *Rob went by plane, but I went by train.*

Wordpower!

Aim: to develop students' topic vocabulary

- Tell students that all the answers appear in the blog they have read.
- Ask students to try to complete the gaps without referring back to the text, but explain that they can if necessary.
- Remind students that they should only write one letter in each gap and that the first letter has been given to help them.
- Encourage them to be careful with their spelling.
- You may also wish to refer students to the *Vocabulary database* on page 139.
- Check the answers orally by asking students to read out the statements and questions.

1 Tourists	4 capital	7 tour
2 sights	5 ticket	8 tour guide
3 traffic	6 view	9 trip

HOMEWORK!

Assign exercises 1–4 on pages 30 and 31 of the Workbook.

Grammar 1

Past simple: basic irregular verbs

Aim: to facilitate students' understanding of the form and usage of the past simple

Warm up!

Aim: to give further practice with present simple and past simple verb tenses

- Write the following words on the board:

ON THE BOARD

did went had saw took gave came got

- Explain to students that these words are all verbs in the past simple.
- Ask students if they know what the present simple of each of these verbs is. You can play a game with this by saying that whoever gets the first one right, can choose another student to do the next one.
- If time permits, ask students to make sentences with some of the verbs.

Grammar presentation 1

- Go through the grammar presentation with students. Check they understand when we use the past simple (to talk about single complete events in the past).
- Explain to students that there is more information on the past simple in *Grammar database 9* on pages 148–149 at the back of the book.
- Ask them to read through the information in the *Grammar database* on their own.
- Ask them if they have any questions.
- Ask students to complete the Quick check task on page 149.
- Check answers orally and ask students to justify their answers, eg *1 Harry was here yesterday.* because we use *was* with singular third person nouns.

Quick check

Circle these correct answers:
1 was
2 take
3 No, I wasn't.
4 see
5 have

1

- Ask students to look at the pictures and then write a sentence using the past simple and the words below each picture.
- Check answers orally and/or by writing them on the board.

2 On Tuesday, Paige had an ice cream.
3 On Wednesday, Paige took some photos.
4 On Thursday, Paige made a sandcastle.
5 On Friday, Paige went up in a helicopter.
6 On Saturday, Paige saw the view from a hill.
7 On Sunday, Paige got a plane ticket home.

2

- Explain to students that they have to complete the gaps by writing the verb in bold in the correct form of the past simple.
- Check answers orally and/or by writing them on the board.

1 was	5 saw	8 did, do
2 didn't have	6 didn't go	9 Were
3 took	7 gave	10 came
4 made		

3

- Ask students to form pairs and ask and answer the questions in exercise 3.
- Encourage them to ask any other questions they can think of, eg *Did you go swimming? Did you take photos? Did you like the food?* etc.
- Go round the class helping students where necessary.

Cool down!

Aim: to review the functions and usage of the past simple

- Ask students to describe their day yesterday, eg *I woke up at seven. I went to school. I saw my friends. I did my homework. I ate dinner. I went to bed.*
- Encourage them to use the negative form of the past simple where possible, eg *I didn't see my friends because I had a test.*

HOMEWORK!

Assign exercises 1–4 on pages 31 and 32 of the Workbook.

Wordpower!

Aim: to develop students' ability to recognise and use the names of continents and countries

1

- Ask students to look at the map and complete the gaps with the names of the continents.
- Encourage students to make a guess if they're not sure.
- You may also wish to refer students to the *Vocabulary database* on page 139.
- Check the answers orally and/or write answers on the board.

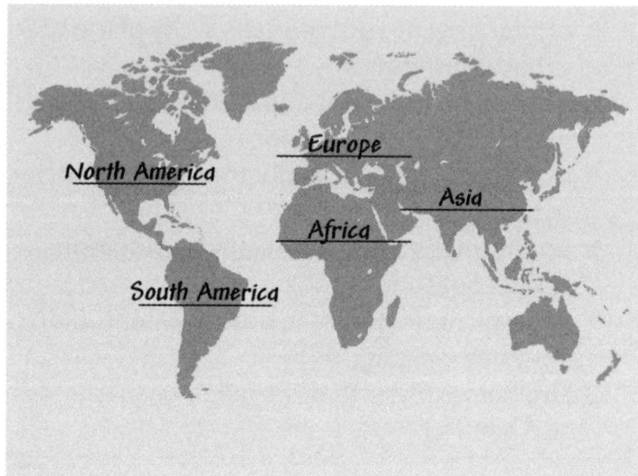

2

- Ask students to look at the countries and place the first letter of each country on the map in the correct location.
- Encourage them to guess if they're not sure.
- Alternatively, you can have students form pairs and help each other locate the countries. You can also do the exercise as a group activity. After the exercise, if time permits, you can ask students where the cities from exercise 3 in the reading section are located.

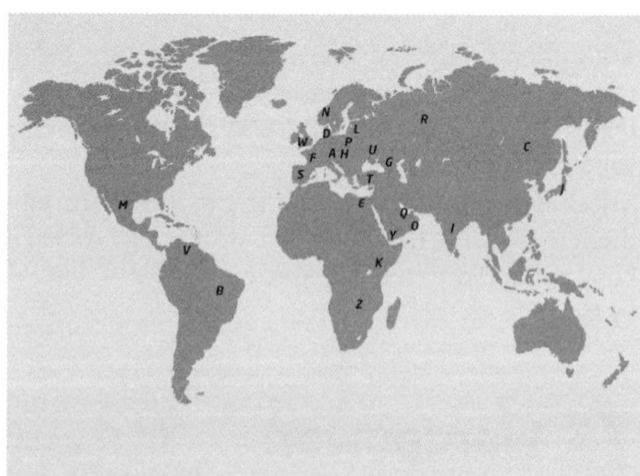

HOMEWORK!

Assign exercises 1 on page 33 of the Workbook.

Listening

Aim: to give practice in listening for gist and specific information

Warm up!

Aim: to introduce the topic of tours

- Ask students to look at the photo.
- Ask simple questions about the photo and elicit responses, eg *What are the people in the photo doing?* (looking at animals), *Where are they?* (Africa), *How are they travelling around?* (in a small bus)

1

- Explain to students that they are going to listen to four people talking about a tour.
- Go through the answer choices and ask students to predict what the people might talk about, eg *I didn't enjoy the hotels. I didn't enjoy the travelling.* etc.
- Ask students to match each person with the thing they didn't enjoy.
- Play the CD track once all the way through. Repeat if necessary.

Speaker 1 a (The hotels weren't very good…)
Speaker 2 c (…but it was just so hot!)
Speaker 3 b (We were on the bus for hours every day, and that was a bit boring.)
Speaker 4 d (He was boring,…)

CD Track 15

2

- Explain to students that they will listen to the recording again.
- Ask them to read through the sentences before they listen, and to predict the answers.
- Play the CD again. Pause when you hear the first correct answer (*two weeks*), and ask students to write it in the gap. Check their answers.
- Play the rest of the recording in its entirety and ask students to listen and work independently to complete the gaps in each of the sentences.
- Check answers together with students. If necessary, play the recording again for students to check incorrect answers.

1 two/2 weeks	5 ten/10
2 animals	6 delicious
3 interesting	7 of the bus
4 (really) friendly	8 phones

CD Track 15

3

- You can either ask students to form pairs and ask and answer the questions in the exercise, or you can do this as a group activity.

Cool down!

Aim: to personalise what the students have listened to

- Ask students what they think makes a good tour. Encourage them to use the answer choices in exercise 1 to talk about the different parts of a tour, eg *A good tour has good, clean hotels. The travelling is easy to do and the weather is nice and warm. The tour guide knows a lot about the places.* etc.

HOMEWORK!

Assign exercises 1 and 2 on page 33 of the Workbook.

Speaking

Aim: to provide practice in talking about travel activities and past events

Warm up!

Aim: to introduce students to basic words and phrases

- Write the following words and phrases on the board:

ON THE BOARD

Last spring First Next Then

- Explain to students that we use these words to relate stories.
- Ask students to give you a sentence to follow *Last spring*, eg *Last spring, I went to Paris.* Continue with the other words on the board.
- You can ask another student to give you another sentence, and continue until you finish, eg *First, I went to the Eiffel Tower. Next, I went shopping. Then, I had a nice meal.* If time permits, you can repeat the task with another set of sentences.

1

- Ask students to look at the pictures and complete the gaps with the names of the sights.
- Encourage them to guess if they're not sure.
- When they have finished, check the answers orally, and/or by writing them on the board.

1 The Empire State Building, New York
2 The Grand Canyon, Arizona
3 Waikiki Beach, Hawaii
4 Disneyland, California
5 SeaWorld, Florida
6 The Rocky Mountains, Colorado

2

- Ask students to look at the activities in exercise 2 and match them with a picture from exercise 1.
- When students have finished, check the answers together orally.

1 Picture 2	4 Picture 6
2 Picture 3	5 Picture 5
3 Picture 4	6 Picture 1

3

- Go through the *Phrase Bank!* with students.
- Ask students to form pairs. Ask them to make a story using the sights and activities from exercises 1 and 2 and tell the story to their partner. When one has finished telling their story, they should swap roles.
- Go round the class helping students where necessary.
- You may also wish to refer students to the *Speaking database* on page 143.

Cool down!

Aim: to give students additional practice with talking about past events

- Ask students to talk about something they did last summer. It can be a visit to a place outside of town, or a place in their town, eg *Last summer, I went to the zoo.*
- Encourage students to use the words from the *Phrase Bank!* to tell their story.

SoundSpot

Aim: to give practice with pronouncing the stress used in names of countries

1

- Check that students know the words *syllable* and *stressed.*
- Ask students to look at the names of the countries and guess how we say each of them.
- Encourage them to say the words aloud, but don't correct their pronunciation or answers at this stage.
- Play the recording and then check students' answers.

Austria	Japan	Russia
Brazil	Kenya	Spain
China	Latvia	Turkey
Denmark	Mexico	Ukraine
Egypt	Norway	Venezuela
France	Oman	Wales
Georgia	Poland	Yemen
Hungary	Qatar	Zimbabwe
India		

CD Track 16

2

- Ask students to listen again, and to repeat the words as they hear them.
- Remind them to be careful to say the correct stress in each of the names of the countries.

CD Track 17

Additional Task

- You can also practise pronouncing the names of the US states in exercise 1 in the speaking section, the continents from the *Wordpower!* on page 45 and/or the cities in exercise 3 in the reading section. You can play a game by asking a student to try to pronounce a word. If they pronounce it correctly, they can choose another student to pronounce the next one.
- Additionally, you can ask students to underline the stressed syllable for each of these additional words.

Grammar 2 G

Past simple: regular verbs and more irregular verbs

Aim: to facilitate students' understanding of the form and use of regular verbs in the past tense and learn additional irregular verbs

Warm up!

Aim: to practise talking about single complete events that happened in the past

- Write on the board:

ON THE BOARD

What did you do yesterday?
I ________ breakfast and ________ TV.
I ________ a museum and ________ at paintings.

- Ask students to look at the sentences and try to guess what present simple verb goes in each of the gaps (eat, watch, visit, look). Then ask students what the verbs are in the past simple. Also, ask students which ones are regular (*watched, visited, looked*) and why (because they take *-ed*) and which one is irregular (*eat*) and why (because it doesn't take *-ed*).
- You can also ask students to change the sentences into the negative form.

Grammar presentation 2

- Go through the grammar presentation with students. Check they understand when we use the past simple.
- Explain to students that there is more information in *Grammar database 10* on page 149 at the back of the book.
- Ask them to read through the information in the *Grammar database* on their own.
- Ask them if they have any questions.
- Ask students to complete the Quick check task on page 149.
- Check answers orally and ask students to justify their answers, eg *1 Did you fly to Paris?* because with questions in the past simple we use *did* + subject + main verb in the infinitive.

Quick check

Circle these correct answers:
1 fly
2 ate
3 Yes, we did.
4 left
5 played

1

- Ask students to look at the table and write the past simple of each of the verbs.
- When students have finished, check the answers together.

arrived	lived	told
drove	looked	travelled
ate	said	watched
found	stopped	wrote

2

- Ask students to read the text and use the verbs from the table in exercise 1 to complete the gaps. Explain that more than one word is possible for one of the gaps.
- When students have finished, check the answers together orally.
- You can also assign one or two students to read out the postcard.

1 drove	5 drove/travelled
2 stopped	6 arrived
3 watched	7 looked
4 ate	8 found

3

- Ask students to complete the gaps by putting the verbs in the box into the past simple.
- Remind students that some of the answers will require the question form.
- When students have finished, check the answers together.
- Assign students to read out the dialogue. Time permitting, repeat with as many students as possible.

1 did, arrive	4 stayed	7 left
2 flew	5 met	8 enjoyed
3 Did, travel	6 made	9 rained

Cool down!

Aim: to review the form of the past simple

- Ask students to think of some other verbs and change them into the past simple. Explain that they can look in Rob's blog from the reading section to find verbs from there that haven't been covered yet (*feel, hope, believe, drop, explore*, etc). Write both the present simple and past simple forms of the verbs on the board and ask students to say if they are regular or irregular.

HOMEWORK!

Assign exercises 1–5 on pages 34 and 35 of the Workbook.

Writing

Aim: to develop the skills necessary to write a blog post

Warm up!

Aim: to familiarise students with the concept of blog posts

- Ask students if they have read a blog on the internet.
- Ask students what personal information people write in their blogs.
- Accept all suggestions at this point, though allow students to disagree with each other if they want to.

1

- Ask students to read the blog silently and individually, and then to choose the correct answers, A, B or C.
- Check answers together when students have finished.

1 A	2 B	3 C

2

- Ask students to read the blog again and match each part of the blog with a statement.
- Check answers together when students have finished.

1 C	3 G	5 A	7 B
2 D	4 E	6 F	

Language Lab

Aim: to focus on key language skills required to achieve this kind of writing task

- Ask students to read the statements aloud.
- Check their understanding of words such as 'exclamation marks', 'emotion', etc before they attempt the task.
- You may wish students to find and underline the examples individually, or to work together as a class.

1 A Wonderful Tour
2 I went to bed and dreamed about India!... We saw the Taj Mahal!... And the food in India was delicious!... visit me at home and she said yes!
3 We got back... It took us a long time... ...we were all very tired when we arrived. I went to bed... ...we travelled all around the country. We visited lots of places, and we stayed in some fantastic hotels. We saw the Taj Mahal! ... I met some very nice people, and I made friends with one girl... We talked about our lives... I asked her... I took lots of photographs. I thought it was a wonderful tour...
4 we were all very tired... ...we stayed in some fantastic hotels... And the food in India was delicious! ...some very nice people... ...a wonderful tour... ...a very beautiful country...

Cool down!

Aim: to personalise what the students have just read

- Ask students what they found interesting about Olivia's tour and her experiences.
- Encourage them to give reasons.
- Ask them what they would like to do or not like to do that Olivia did, eg *I would like to see the Taj Mahal, too. I wouldn't like to eat chicken curry.* etc.

HOMEWORK!

Assign exercises 1 and 2 on page 35 of the Workbook.

Plan your project!

Aim: to guide students through the writing process

1

- Explain to students that they are going to write a blog similar to Olivia's.
- First, ask students to look at the pictures and decide which country belongs with which picture.
- Check answers together when students have finished.

1 China	3 the USA
2 England	4 Brazil

2

- Ask students to imagine they just got back from a trip.
- Explain that for each of the questions in exercise 2, they will write a short piece of information to answer the question.
- Encourage students to use their imagination when answering the questions.

3

- Explain to students that they are going to complete the *Planner.*
- Point to the first column and explain that these are the different parts of the blog.
- Point to the second column and explain that this is useful information about each part.
- Ask the students to make notes for each of the parts in the third column. Encourage them to write two or three things for each of the paragraphs.
- Encourage them to use their imagination.
- Check their planners before moving on to exercise 4.

4

- You may wish to assign this for homework or, if there's time, for the students to do this in class.
- Explain to students that they are going to use their notes from the *Planner* in exercise 3 to write their blog.
- Explain to them that using their notes is not cheating and that it is important to make a detailed plan before you start writing.
- Allow them to look back at Olivia's blog if they're not sure what to do. At this stage, the most important thing is that the students create a successful piece of writing.
- You may also wish them to consult the *Writing database* on page 135, which has a further model to study.
- You may wish to encourage stronger students to take risks with their writing, but it's probably best if weaker students follow the model completely.
- Encourage the students to add photos or drawings to their blog if they like.
- You may wish to comment on the students' writing before they produce a final version.

Additional Tasks and Tests

- Student's CD-ROM: Unit 5
- Teacher's DVD-ROM: Unit 5 Test
- Teacher's DVD-ROM: Term Test 1 (Units 1–5)
- Teacher's DVD-ROM Test Generator: Unit 5

6

Animal Magic!

Target language

Reading skills: reading for gist / specific information (matching to make questions, T/F/DS)
Vocabulary: topic vocabulary (animals), general basic vocabulary (ways of moving)
Grammar: regular and irregular plurals, articles
Listening skills: listening for gist / specific information (multiple matching, text completion)
Speaking skills: giving simple instructions
Pronunciation skills: stress in 2- or 3-syllable words
Writing skills: note (giving instructions)

Get ready!

Aim: to learn and use words for people and parts of the body

- Ask students to look at the picture and label each of the people and parts as shown.
- You may wish to refer students to the *Vocabulary database* on page 139.
- Review answers together orally.
- You may wish to point out other body parts that were not labelled and ask students to say what they are.

1 adult (man)	5 adult (woman)
2 mouth	6 foot/feet
3 tooth/teeth	7 child
4 tongue	

Reading

Aim: to introduce the topic of strange animal facts

Warm up!

Aim: to talk about the difference between rumours and facts

- Write the following words and phrases on the board:

ON THE BOARD

newspaper article internet article advert teacher online chat room

- Explain that a fact is a piece of information that is proven to be true, while a rumour is a piece of information that is not proven to be true.
- Ask students to look at the board and say which sources are more likely to have rumours and which are more likely to have facts.

1

- Choose a few volunteers to read each paragraph of the magazine article aloud.
- Encourage them to ignore all unknown vocabulary at this stage.
- Start by reading the disclaimer in the pink box.
- Give students a short time to match each paragraph with a photo; explain to students that one photo won't be used.
- Review the answers together before moving on.

1 c	2 a	3 e	4 b

2

- Give students a short time to make questions by choosing correct phrases from the list a–e.
- Check the answers together orally.

1 c	2 a	3 e	4 b	5 d

3

- Ask students to quickly read through the statements and identify any unknown vocabulary (eg they may not know that *stuck* in number 5 is the past participle of the verb *stick*).
- Ask students to read the article again, this time to themselves.
- Give them a short time to identify whether each statement is true (T), false (F) or whether it doesn't say anything about the statement in the article (DS).
- Review the answers together orally. Encourage students to justify their answers by giving reasons.

1 T (In fact, it seems that goldfish can remember things for at least three months.)
2 F (They don't use a mouth like we do. They use their feet!)
3 DS
4 DS
5 F (…it's stuck to the bottom of its mouth.)
6 T (Their teeth are very sharp (of course!) but they fall out all the time – even when they're adults.)
7 F (A crocodile usually has about 70 teeth in its mouth…)
8 DS
9 T (Did you know … that in real life Walt Disney was scared of mice?)

4

- Ask students to think about the strange facts they learned from reading the article.
- Give them a short time to answer the question by noting down one thing they learned.
- You may want to encourage stronger students to do this task without looking back at the text.
- Ask each student to share his/her sentence by reading it aloud.

Cool down!

Aim: to give more practice in talking about strange facts

- Ask students to think about other strange facts they have learned from various sources.
- Invite students to take turns telling the class about the strange fact they find most interesting.
- Ask them to tell the class what the source of the information was, eg newspaper article, internet, teacher, family member, etc.

HOMEWORK!

Assign exercises 1–5 on pages 36 and 37 of the Workbook.

Wordpower!

Aim: to develop students' topic vocabulary

- Tell students that all the answers are in the magazine article they have read.
- Ask them to try filling in the gaps to complete each word without referring back to the text, but explain that they can if they need to.
- Remind students they should write only one letter in each gap and that the first letter has been given to help them.
- Remind them to be careful with their spelling.
- You may wish to refer students to the *Vocabulary database* on page 139.
- Check the answers together orally.

1 fact	3 lick	5 lifetime
2 memory	4 grow	6 cute, sweet

Additional Task

- Ask students to think about strange animal behaviours they have either heard about or seen first-hand.
- Give them a short time to note down the animal's behaviour, but not name the animal.
- Invite them to take turns reading their strange animal facts. As a student reads his/her strange fact, the rest of the class will guess what animal the student is describing.

Grammar 1 G

Regular and irregular plurals

Aim: to facilitate students' understanding of the formation and usage of the regular and irregular plurals

Warm up!

Aim: to give practice using regular plurals to talk about animal groups

- Write the following words on the board:

ON THE BOARD

bird	*birds*
crocodile	*crocodiles*
butterfly	*butterflies*

My favourite animal is the ___________.
There are many things to learn about ___________.

- Use the words on the board to demonstrate regular plurals.
- Ask students to choose one of the animals listed on the board and complete the sentences using the singular and plural verbs.
- Have them write their sentences down on paper and then read them aloud.

Grammar presentation 1

- Go through the grammar presentation with students.
- Review the uses of regular and irregular plurals.
- Explain that most nouns add *-s* to form the plural, but there are special rules for nouns ending in a consonant + *-y*, nouns ending in *-ch*/sh and nouns ending in *-x*.
- Review examples of irregular nouns.
- Explain that there are more examples and additional information on regular and irregular plurals in *Grammar database 11* on page 149 at the back of the book.
- Ask students to read through the information in the *Grammar database* on their own.
- Ask them if they have questions.
- Assign students the Quick check task on page 149.

- Check answers orally and ask students to justify their answers, eg *1 cherries* because nouns ending in a consonant + *-y* change to *–ies*.

Quick check

Circle these correct answers:
1 cherries
2 watches
3 boxes
4 sheep
5 children

1

- Ask students to choose the correct form – regular or irregular – of the words in bold to fill in each gap.
- Check answers together orally.

1 mice	5 teeth, hands
2 children, lions	6 flies, cherries
3 men, women, puppies	7 fish(es), boys
4 sheep, boxes	

2

- Put students into pairs, or allow them to choose a partner.
- Explain that they're going to look at the pictures together and ask each other the question *What's happening in this picture?*
- Students will take turns being Student A, the one who asks the question, and Student B, the one who provides short answers.

Suggested answers:
2 Four children are looking at two lions.
3 A man and two women are playing with two puppies.
4 Four sheep are jumping over two boxes.
5 A boy is holding a tooth in his hands.
6 Four flies are sitting on some cherries.
7 Five fish are swimming below two boys.

Cool down!

Aim: to give students additional practice with irregular plurals

- Write the following words on the board:

ON THE BOARD

man woman child mouse goose foot tooth

- Ask a student to use a singular form of a word from the board to tell the class something interesting, eg *I saw a mouse in my house last night.*
- Ask a second student to respond by making his/her statement more impressive using the plural form of the same word, eg *I saw two mice in my house last night.*
- Continue until all the words are used. Allow students to use any plural amount they would like and have some fun with it, eg *I saw a thousand mice in my house last night!*

HOMEWORK!

Assign exercises 1–4 on pages 37 and 38 of the Workbook.

Wordpower!

Aim: to develop students' topic vocabulary

1

- Tell students that all the words in bold describe the ways that people and animals move.
- Ask them to pay close attention to the names of animals as they try matching the sentences to the pictures. Explain they will use one of the pictures three times.
- You may wish to refer students to the *Vocabulary database* on page 139.
- Review answers together orally.

a 3	c 4	e 6/7/8
b 1	d 2	f 5

2

- Give students a short time to review the cartoon and choose the correct word to describe what the people are doing.
- Review answers together orally.

1 pull	2 picked	3 putting

Additional Task

Aim: to give additional practice using words to describe movement

- Mime an action and ask students to guess what you are doing by shouting out a word or phrase from exercise 1.

HOMEWORK!

Assign exercises 1 and 2 on page 39 of the Workbook.

Listening

Aim: to give practice in listening for gist and specific information

Warm up!

Aim: to develop skills in listening to instructions

- Put students into pairs, or allow them to choose a partner.
- Ask Student A to note down a type of animal, but not tell Student B.
- Student A will describe the animal to Student B, who will sketch a picture of the animal based on Student A's description, eg *four legs, floppy ears, long hair,* etc.

- When Student B is finished, he/she will show the sketch to Student A, who will reveal the animal he/she noted down. The students will see how closely the picture matches the animal.
- When finished, ask the students to swap roles and repeat the exercise.

1

- Explain to students they will be listening to someone describing two of the animals in the pictures.
- Ask students to look at the three pictures as they listen.
- As students listen, ask them to choose the correct picture for each animal that is described.
- Play the CD track once all the way through.
- Review answers orally together.

1 c	2 a

CD Track 18

2

- Explain to students they will listen to the recording again.
- Ask students to fill in the gaps as they listen.
- Play the CD track once all the way through. Repeat if necessary.
- Review answers orally together.

1 ears	4 finger	7 head
2 mice	5 pulls	8 mouth
3 teeth	6 humans	

CD Track18

3

- Ask students to talk about themselves by answering the questions about their pet preferences.
- Allow students to ask and answer these questions in pairs or as a group if you prefer.
- Go round the class helping students where necessary.

Cool down!

Aim: to give additional practice with describing animals

- Ask students to imagine they are zookeepers at the *Zany Zoo*, which is filled with strange and unusual animals.
- Ask them to describe the zaniest animal in the *Zany Zoo*, say what it likes to eat, and describe how it likes to spend its day.

HOMEWORK!

Assign exercises 1 and 2 on page 39 of the Workbook.

Speaking

Aim: to give practice in giving simple instructions

Warm up!

Aim: to introduce the topic of caring for a pet

- Ask students to imagine they are describing their pet to the class. If they do not have one, they can make one up.
- Invite students to say what their pet needs to be happy.
- Give an example to get them started, eg *Spot needs to run every day.*

1

- Put students into pairs, or allow them to choose a partner.
- Explain that they're going to listen to a dialogue between a pet shop owner and a customer.
- Play the CD track once all the way through.
- Now ask each student pair to read the dialogue, with one student playing the role of the pet shop owner and one playing the role of the customer.
- When they have gone through the dialogue, they should swap roles.

CD Track 19

2

- Students should remain in pairs to do the role-play. They will keep their roles as pet shop owner and customer, but this time the pet shop owner will give the customer instructions on how to care for a pet python.
- Encourage students to use the notes to help them in their role-play.
- Go through the *Phrase Bank!* with students and talk about the style of speaking when giving instructions.
- You may also wish to refer students to the *Speaking database* on page 143.
- When they have finished, students can swap roles and repeat the exercise.

Cool down!

Aim: to give students additional practice with giving instructions

- Ask students to remain in pairs, but this time they will give their partners instructions on how to care for their own pets. If they do not have one, they can make one up.
- Go round the class helping students where necessary.

SoundSpot

Aim: to give practice in saying 2- and 3-syllable words with the proper stresses

1

- Encourage the students to say the words aloud, but don't correct their pronunciation at this stage.
- Explain to the students that as they listen, they should underline the correct syllable to show which part of the word is stressed the most.
- Play the recording and then check students' answers.

women	python	puppy
children	gecko	kitten
crocodile	butterfly	goldfish

CD Track 20

2

- Ask students to listen again to the recording and repeat the words.
- Remind them to be careful of which syllables they stress.

CD Track 21

Grammar 2

Articles
Aim: to facilitate students' understanding of the functions and usage of articles

Warm up!

Aim: to introduce the concept of articles

- Write the following words on the board:

ON THE BOARD

a an the

- Explain to students that articles are non-descriptive words that come before a noun.
- Say that you're going to read the sentences in the *Grammar 2* introduction on page 55, but that you're going to read the sentences without the articles.
- Ask students to listen as you read out the sentences, and to put up their hand as soon as they notice an article is missing.
- Ask students to identify the missing article.

Grammar presentation 2

- Go through the grammar presentation with students. Check they understand when we use *a* (with singular nouns that begin with a consonant sound when we are not being specific), *an* (with singular nouns that begin with a vowel sound when we are not being specific), *the* (with singular and plural nouns when we are being specific, and certain place names) and no article (with plural nouns when we are not being specific, and certain other place names).
- Explain to students there is more information on articles in *Grammar database 12* on page 150 at the back of the book.
- Ask them to read through the information in the *Grammar database* on their own.
- Ask them if they have any questions.
- Ask students to complete the Quick check task on page 150.
- Check answers together orally and ask students to justify their answers, eg *1 a dog* because *dog* is a singular noun.

Quick check

Circle these correct answers:
1 a dog
2 a very big car
3 Elephants
4 an
5 the weekend

1

- Ask students to do their best to choose the appropriate article in each sentence, based on the rules they have studied.
- After they have filled in the gaps, have them listen to the conversation between Jake and Zak. Invite them to change their answers, if needed, as they listen to the recording.
- Review answers together orally.

1 an 2 a 3 an 4 a 5 a

CD Track 22

2

- Ask students to read each line of the dialogue and decide whether the article *the* is needed.
- Remind them that in some sentences the article *the* is not required, in which case they should choose the dash.
- After they have filled in the gaps, have them listen to the conversation between Jake and Zak. Invite them to change their answers, if needed, as they listen to the recording.
- Review answers together orally.

1 the	4 the	6 –	8 –	10 The
2 –	5 –	7 the	9 the	11 the
3 –				

CD Track 23

3

- Ask students to read each line of the dialogue and decide whether the articles *the*, *a* or *an* are needed.
- Remind them that in some sentences an article is not required, in which case they should choose the dash.
- After they have filled in the gaps, ask them to listen to the conversation between Jake and Zak.
- Invite them to change their answers, if needed, as they listen to the recording.
- Review answers together orally, pointing out for item 3 that although they heard *an* in the recording, *the* is also correct.

1 a	3 an/the	5 –	7 –
2 the	4 a	6 –	

CD Track 24

Cool down!

Aim: to review the functions and usage of articles

- Write the following scrambled sentences on the board:

ON THE BOARD

to I going am cinema ______
cat ______ have We
important is maths It study ______ to

- Refer students to the scrambled sentences on the board.
- Give them a short time to put the words in the proper order to create full sentences.
- Explain that the ______ represents a missing article, which they will need to fill in to complete the sentence.
- Explain that, in one of the sentences on the board, no article is needed.
- Remind students to add punctuation.
- Review answers together orally. (Answers: *I am going to the cinema. We have a cat. It is important to study maths.*)

HOMEWORK!

Assign exercises 1–4 on pages 40 and 41 of the Workbook.

Writing

Aim: to develop skills necessary to write simple instructions

Warm up!

Aim: to familiarise students with language used in giving instructions

- Write the following words on the board:

ON THE BOARD

Give me Tell your Don't forget

- Refer students to the phrases on the board.
- Ask volunteers to give an instruction by starting a sentence with one of the phrases, eg *Tell your brother to call me.*

1

- Ask students to read the note quietly to themselves. Explain that they should think about who might be writing the note and who is meant to read the note.
- Give them a short time to write the correct words or phrases.
- Review answers together orally.

1 Adrian
2 Linda
3 look after Adrian's/his pets
4 to help her
5 4/four
6 call him/Adrian
7 (on) Sunday evening

2

- Ask students to read the note again.
- Check they know the meanings of *once* (= one time) and *twice* (= two times).
- Give them a short time to match the phrases to make sentences.
- Review answers together orally and ask students to justify their answers based on references in the note.

1 c	3 a	5 f
2 e	4 b	6 d

Language Lab

Aim: to focus on key language found in a note that gives simple instructions

- Check students' understanding of phrases typically used to give instructions, eg *Do this, Do that, Don't forget to, Don't do this, Never do that, You can,* etc before beginning the tasks.
- You may wish students to find and underline the examples individually, or to work together as a class.

1
Feed the cat three times a day (in the morning, at lunchtime and in the evening).
Feed the dog twice a day.
Take the dog for a walk once or twice a day.
Make sure the cat and dog have a bowl of water.
Say hello to the parrot.
Play with the gecko.
Make sure the gecko's box is clean.
2
Don't forget to call me if you have any problems!
3
...but don't let it leave its cage.
...but never pull its tail!
4
You can pick it up...

Cool down!

Aim: to give extra practice in giving simple instructions

- Ask students if they ever had to take care of anything (pet, plant, younger brother/sister, etc) for someone else.
- Ask them to tell the class what their responsibilities were and how they felt about doing them.

HOMEWORK!

Assign exercises 1 and 2 on page 41 of the Workbook.

Plan your project!

Aim: to guide students through the process of writing instructions for looking after a pet

1

- Explain to students that they're going to write down instructions for a pet sitter who will take care of their pet while they are on holiday.
- Ask them to think of four different pets; encourage them to use their imagination!
- Give students a short time to write down their four different pets.

2

- Ask students to keep using their imagination to answer the questions about their pet's needs.
- Explain they will use this information to begin writing their instructions.

3

- Explain to students that they are going to complete the *Planner*.
- Point to the first column and explain that these are the main parts of the note they will write to their pet sitter.
- Point to the second column and explain that this is useful information about each part.
- Ask the students to write as much information as they can (in note form) in the third column.
- Check their planners before moving on to exercise 4.

4

- You may wish to assign this for homework or, if there's time, have the students do this in class.
- Explain to students that they're going to use their notes from the *Planner* in exercise 3 to write their note to the pet sitter.
- Invite them to look back at Adrian's note to Linda to help guide them through the exercise.
- You may also wish them to consult the *Writing database* on page 136, which has a further model to study.
- Remind students to use a friendly tone in their writing.
- You may wish to encourage stronger students to take risks with their writing, but it's probably best if weaker students follow the model completely.
- You may wish to comment on the students' writing before they produce a final version.

Additional Tasks and Tests

- Page 157: Units 5–6 Song
- Student's CD-ROM: Unit 6
- Teacher's DVD-ROM: Unit 6 Test
- Teacher's DVD-ROM Test Generator: Unit 6

Units 5-6 Revision

You may wish to use this section in any of the following ways with your class:

As a test

- Advise students a few days in advance that they should review the language from Units 5 and 6.
- Before beginning, go through the instructions for each exercise, making sure students understand what is required of them.
- Give students approximately 30 minutes to complete the exercises in test conditions.
- Collect students' books and mark the tests yourself, handing them back the following lesson. Alternatively, go over the answers in the same lesson and ask students to swap books with their partner and mark each other's work.
- The total number of marks for the test is 49 and the following should be taken as a rough guide to students' performance:

44 and over: Brilliant!
40 to 43: Very good!
35 to 39: Good!
26 to 34: Could be better …
25 or under: Should be better …

As homework

- Assign all of the exercises after Units 5 and 6 have been completed.
- Go through the instructions for each exercise as you assign them, making sure students understand what is required of them.
- You may want to ask students to complete this section without referring back to the units at all.
- Check answers in class orally, or by writing them on the board.

As classwork

- You may wish to use exercises from this section as supplementary material if you feel that a certain language area needs more work.
- Select the exercises which you feel best suit your students' needs and assign them either as pair work or to be done alone.

1

1 ferry
2 traffic
3 view
4 carriage
5 sights
6 guide
7 ticket
8 capital

2

1 run
2 drop
3 up
4 down
5 jump
6 pushed

3

1 Hungary
2 Brazil
3 Austria
4 Kenya
5 Europe
6 Denmark
7 Norway

					A	U	S	T	R	I	A
D	E	N	M	A	R	K					
	H	U	N	G	A	R	Y				
		N	O	R	W	A	Y				
		B	R	A	Z	I	L				
				K	E	N	Y	A			
	E	U	R	O	P	E					

4

1 had
2 went
3 flew
4 met
5 found
6 took
7 showed
8 ate
9 drove
10 saw
11 left
12 was

5

1 mice
2 teeth
3 women
4 sheep
5 children
6 boxes
7 babies
8 watches

6

1 a
2 the
3 –
4 the
5 a
6 the
7 an
8 –

7

At the Airport!

Target language

Reading skills:	reading for gist / specific information (multiple matching, T/F)
Vocabulary:	topic vocabulary (travelling by plane), general basic vocabulary (materials)
Grammar:	countable and uncountable nouns, quantitative adjectives (*some, any, many, much, a lot of, no*)
Listening skills:	listening for gist / specific information (multiple choice questions, sentence completion)
Speaking skills:	talking about travelling by plane, agreeing and disagreeing
Pronunciation skills:	pronunciation of hard and soft *g*
Writing skills:	description of a scene

Get ready!

Aim: to learn and use phrases to talk about travelling by plane

- Ask students if any of them have been on a plane, then ask what they took with them, eg *clothes, bags, money, plane tickets,* etc. If no one has been on a plane, ask them to imagine what they would bring. Additionally, you can ask students what they can do while they're on a plane, eg *read, sleep, watch a film, eat, listen to music,* etc.
- Ask students to look at the picture and give them a short time to label the picture with the words in the box.
- You may wish to refer students to the *Vocabulary database* on page 139.
- Check answers orally and/or write the numbers of the different parts of the picture on the board with the correct words.

1 pilot	3 wing	5 airport
2 passenger	4 engine	

Reading

Aim: to give practice in reading for gist and specific information

Warm up!

Aim: to introduce the concept of airport jobs and their descriptions

- Ask students to imagine what kinds of things an airport worker does, eg *takes people's bags, helps them find their plane, takes their plane tickets, takes bags from one plane to another,* etc.
- Accept all suggestions at this point, though allow students to disagree with each other if they want to.

1

- Ask students to silently and individually read the text. Encourage them to ignore all unknown vocabulary at this stage.
- Ask students some very general and simple questions about the text, eg *What kind of text is this?* (an article), *Who is it about?* (people who work at airports), *What is the article about?* (airport jobs), etc.
- Give students a few minutes to do exercise 1. Go round the class helping students where necessary.
- Check answers orally and/or write answers on the board.

1 J	3 J	5 N
2 R	4 N	6 R

2

- Encourage students to do this task quickly but carefully (to help develop their scanning skills).
- Tell students they should decide whether each statement is true or false by circling 'T' or 'F'.
- Encourage students to underline in the text where they find the answer.
- When they have finished, discuss the answers together. Encourage students to justify their answers by giving reasons.

1 T (Every time a plane lands, a mechanic like me checks that everything's fine.)
2 T (I check the wings carefully and tell the pilot that it's safe to fly.)
3 F (I explain to passengers how to stay safe on a plane,…)
4 T (To be a good flight attendant, you need to have a good smile and enjoy helping people.)
5 F (Sometimes someone brings their wife's or husband's passport by mistake, but we can't let them travel, I'm afraid.)
6 F (We put all the bags through a scanner so that we can see inside them.)

3

- Ask students to form pairs, or allow them to choose their own partner.
- Explain that they're going to ask each other questions about airport travel.
- Ask one student in each pair to ask the questions in exercise 3 and note down the other student's replies.
- When the student has asked all the questions, they should swap roles.
- You may wish to encourage them to ask one additional question which is not on the list.

Cool down!

Aim: to encourage students to talk about airports in general

- Ask students to talk about what things about an airport or travelling by plane they think are interesting or exciting, eg *It's interesting that there are many people in an airport from many different countries. It's exciting to fly because the plane goes very fast.* etc.

Wordpower!

Aim: to develop students' topic vocabulary

- Tell students that all the answers appear in the article they have read.
- Ask students to try to complete the gaps without referring back to the text, but explain that they can if necessary.
- Remind students that they should only write one letter in each gap and that the first letter has been given to help them.
- Encourage them to be careful with their spelling.
- You may wish to refer students to the *Vocabulary database* on page 139.
- Check the answers orally by asking students to read out the sentences.

1 catch	4 passengers	7 passport
2 take off	5 safe	8 baggage
3 land	6 emergency	

HOMEWORK!

Assign exercises 1–4 on pages 43 and 44 of the Workbook.

Grammar 1

Countable and uncountable nouns

Aim: to facilitate students' understanding of the functions and usage of countable and uncountable nouns

Warm up!

Aim: to practise recognising and using countable and uncountable nouns

- Explain to students that they're going to play a game.
- Write the following words on the board:

ON THE BOARD

bag money passport food music book hat water

- Ask students to imagine they're going on a plane. Ask a student to finish the sentence, *I'm going on a plane and I'm taking…*, using three of the words from the board as items.
- Encourage students to use singular and plural forms of countable nouns and to use uncountable nouns, eg *I'm going on a plane and I'm taking two bags, money and a book.*
- Time permitting, you can continue the game with students coming up with their own ideas for items to take on the plane.

Grammar presentation 1

- Go through the grammar presentation with students. Check they understand what countable and uncountable nouns are (some nouns are countable and have a plural, some nouns are uncountable and don't have a plural).
- Explain to students that there is more information on countable and uncountable nouns in *Grammar database 13* on page 150 at the back of the book.
- Ask them to read through the information in the *Grammar database* on their own.
- Ask them if they have any questions.
- Ask students to complete the Quick check task on page 150.
- Check answers orally and ask students to justify their answers, eg *1 The information is correct.* because *information* is an uncountable noun, so we use *is*.

Quick check

Circle these correct answers:
1 is
2 food
3 pop music
4 water
5 advice

1

- Explain to students that they have to complete the gaps with the correct form of each of the nouns.
- Check answers orally and/or by writing them on the board.

1 hair	3 planes	5 trips
2 fruit	4 work	6 passengers

2

- Explain to students that they have to tick the correct sentences and underline the mistakes in the incorrect sentences and write the correct word.
- Check answers orally and/or by writing them on the board.

1 Don't leave your baggages alone in the airport. (baggage)
2 ✓
3 ✓
4 I got some informations about how you become a flight attendant. (information)
5 Lots of people were asleep on the furnitures in the airport. (furniture)
6 They usually play relaxing musics in airports. (music)

3

- Ask students to read the text and choose the correct word to complete the sentences.
- When students have finished, check their answers together. Ask a student to read the text aloud.

1 gentlemen	6 advice is
2 information	7 attendants are
3 metres	8 food
4 kilometres	9 drinks
5 hours	

Cool down!

Aim: to review the functions and usage of countable and uncountable nouns

- Ask students to look around the classroom and find four or five things that are countable, eg *In the classroom we have desks, chairs, books, pens and pencils.* Then ask students to try to find four or five things in the classroom that are uncountable, eg *In the classroom we have furniture, paper and rubbish.*
- You can write these words on the board and/or ask students to write them down in their notebooks in two columns, one column for countable nouns and one column for uncountable nouns.

HOMEWORK!

Assign exercises 1–3 on pages 44 and 45 of the Workbook.

Wordpower!

Aim: to develop students' ability to recognise and use words that show what material objects are made of

1

- Ask students to look at the pictures and write a word from the box that shows the material each object is made of. You can also ask students to name the objects before they start the task.
- Encourage students to make a guess if they're not sure.
- You may also wish to refer students to the *Vocabulary database* on page 139.
- Check the answers orally and/or write answers on the board.

1 metal	4 rubber	7 leather
2 plastic	5 glass	8 wood
3 cotton	6 cardboard	

Additional Task

- Write these words on the board:

ON THE BOARD

pencil car shoes table

- Ask students to say what different materials each of these items are made of. Remind students that more than one material is possible, and encourage them to include all the materials that are possible, eg *A pencil is made of wood, metal and rubber. A car is made of metal, glass and plastic.* etc.

2

- Ask students to form pairs. Give each pair a different material and tell them to write it in the table.
- Explain to students that each pair has two minutes to write as many objects as they can think of that are made of that material. Remind them to write the words in English and to use their dictionaries if necessary.
- When they have finished, ask one student in each pair to read out their material and the objects they came up with.

HOMEWORK!

Assign exercises 1 and 2 on page 46 of the Workbook.

Listening

Aim: to give practice in listening for gist and specific information

Warm up!

Aim: to practise listening to a conversation involving travelling by plane

- Ask students to look at the sentences in exercise 1.
- Ask simple questions about the sentences and elicit responses, eg *Where are these two people talking?* (at an airport), *Does the man work in the airport?* (No, he's travelling.) *Does the woman work in the airport?* (Yes)

1

- Explain to students that they are going to listen to someone trying to travel by plane.
- Ask students to choose the correct answer for each item, A, B or C, while they listen to the conversation.
- Play the CD track once all the way through. Repeat if necessary.

1 B (That's where your plane is.)
2 C (It's usually 20 minutes before the plane leaves.)
3 A (I asked for a seat next to the window.)

CD Track 25

2

- Explain to students that they will listen to the recording again.
- Ask them to read through the sentences before they listen, and to predict the answers.
- Play the CD again. Pause when you hear the first correct answer (*Egypt*), and ask students to write it in the gap. Check their answers.
- Play the rest of the recording in its entirety and ask students to listen and work independently to complete the rest of the gaps.
- Check answers together with students. If necessary, play the recording again for students to check incorrect answers.

1 Egypt	3 D13	5 7F
2 217	4 9.30	

CD Track 25

3

- Ask students to look at the picture and to talk about the reasons people are afraid of flying.
- You can ask students to form pairs and discuss these questions with each other, or do the task as a class.

Cool down!

Aim: to personalise what the students have listened to

- Ask students to think of some ways to make travel easy and fun. Assist them with some prompts if necessary, eg ask students *What can we do while we wait for our plane? Read a book, listen to music, play a game with the person we're travelling with.* etc.

HOMEWORK!

Assign exercises 1 and 2 on pages 46 and 47 of the Workbook.

Speaking

Aim: to provide practice in talking about travelling by plane, and agreeing and disagreeing with people

Warm up!

Aim: to introduce students to the different stages of flying

- Ask students to think of the first thing they do when they want to travel by plane. Give an example to students and elicit responses, eg *The first thing we do when we want to travel by plane is go to the airport. Is that correct?*
- Accept all responses at this point, though allow students to disagree with each other if they want to.
- Encourage students to explain their answers, eg *No, that's not correct. We buy the plane tickets first.*

1

- Go through the *Phrase Bank!* with students before you ask students to do exercise 1.
- Ask students to form pairs, look at the pictures and talk with each other about which picture happens first, which picture happens second and so on.
- Go round the class helping students where necessary.
- When they have finished, check the answers orally, and/or write them on the board.

1 c	3 e	5 f
2 d	4 a	6 b

2

- While students are still in pairs, explain to them that they are going to do a role-play.
- Explain to students that one of them is a passenger who's travelling by plane and the other is working at the information desk.
- Once they've decided who plays which role, ask them to read the instructions and the example conversation below the instructions. They should then have a similar conversation.
- When the students have completed their roles, they should swap.
- You may wish to encourage them to ask and answer one additional question which is not in the instructions.
- Go round the class helping students where necessary.

Cool down!

Aim: to give students additional practice with talking about travelling by plane

- Ask students to think about what happens when the plane lands, eg *The first thing you do is get off the plane. The next thing you do is get your bags.* etc.
- Encourage students to use the phrases they learned from the *Phrase Bank!* when there's something that they don't agree with, eg *No, I don't think that's right. The next thing you do is you go through a security check.*

SoundSpot

Aim: to give practice in pronouncing the hard and soft 'g'

1

- Ask students to look at the words and guess how we say each of them.
- Encourage them to say the words aloud, but don't correct their pronunciation or answers at this stage.
- Play the recording and then check students' answers.
- Point out that there are two ways that we pronounce the letter *g*. Additionally, you can ask students if they can tell you when we say a hard 'g' (when the *g* is in front of a consonant or the vowels *a*, *o* and *u*) and when we say a soft 'g' (when the *g* is in front of the vowels *e* and *i*). Explain to students that, rarely, when the *g* is in front of *e* and *i*, such as in the words *girl* and *get*, it is pronounced like a hard 'g'.

A hard 'g' sound	A soft 'g' sound (like 'j')
glass	emergency
gate	engine
bag	baggage
baggage	dangerous
ground	passenger
guard	

CD Track 26

2

- Ask students to listen again, and to repeat the words as they hear them.
- Remind them to be careful how they say the *g* in each word.

CD Track 27

Additional Task

- Ask students to think of some people's names that have a *g* in them, eg *George, Gina, Gary, Angela.* Use the names of students in class that have a *g* in them also.
- Alternatively, you can ask students to think of any other words that have a *g* and write the words on the board in a table as exercise 1.

Grammar 2 G

Quantitative adjectives (*some, any, many, much, a lot of, no*)

Aim: to facilitate students' understanding of the functions and usage of quantitative adjectives

Warm up!

Aim: to talk about amounts of things when they are countable nouns or uncountable nouns

- Write on the board:

ON THE BOARD

	Billy	Georgia
bags:	2 bags	5 bags
money:	2 euros	200 euros
food:	none	an apple

- Explain to students that the two people on the board, Billy and Georgia, are flying together today.
- Ask students to talk about the items that Billy and Georgia have got using the quantitative adjectives *some, any, many, much, a lot of* and *no*, eg *Billy has got some bags, but Georgia has got a lot of bags.* Assist students with making sentences when necessary.
- Encourage students to use negative sentences as well, eg *Billy hasn't got much money, but Georgia has got a lot of money. Billy hasn't got any food, but Georgia has got some food.*

Grammar presentation 2

- Go through the grammar presentation with students. Check they understand when we use quantitative adjectives.
- Explain to students that there is more information in *Grammar database 14* on page 150 at the back of the book.
- Ask them to read through the information in the *Grammar database* on their own.
- Ask them if they have any questions.
- Ask students to complete the Quick check task on page 150.
- Check answers orally and ask students to justify their answers, eg *1 I've got some free time.* because we use *some* with affirmative statements.

Quick check

Circle these correct answers:
1 some
2 no
3 any
4 much
5 many

1

- Ask students to look at the phrases in exercise 1 and to cross out the ones that are incorrect.
- When students have finished, check the answers together.

1 some passengers	6 many flights
2 ~~much flight attendants~~	7 no baggage
3 ~~many fruit~~	8 ~~many work~~
4 a lot of money	9 many jobs
5 no information	10 any bags

2

- Ask students to complete the exercise by choosing the correct word or phrase to complete each sentence.
- When students have finished, check the answers together orally.

1 many	4 no	7 a lot of
2 a lot of	5 any	8 many
3 much	6 any	

3

- Ask students to read the text and to complete the exercise by putting the correct quantitative adjective into each gap.
- Remind students that they will use some of the words or phrases more than once, and that there is more than one answer for some gaps.
- When students have finished, check the answers together.
- Assign students to read out the text. Time permitting, repeat with as many students as possible.

1 a lot of/many	5 much/a lot of
2 no	6 any
3 A lot of	7 any
4 some	8 no

Cool down!

Aim: to review the functions and usage of quantitative adjectives

- Ask students to look at exercise 1 again.
- For the phrases that students found to be wrong, ask them to make sentences with the correct form of the phrase, eg *There are many flight attendants on a large plane.* etc.
- Encourage students to form negative sentences, eg *There isn't much fruit in the kitchen.*
- If time permits, ask students to form sentences and questions with the other phrases in the exercise.

HOMEWORK!

Assign exercises 1–4 on pages 47 and 48 of the Workbook.

Writing

Aim: to develop the skills necessary to write a description of a scene

Warm up!

Aim: to familiarise students with the concept of descriptions

- Ask students if they have ever visited a museum and looked at a painting of people who are outdoors.
- Ask students what kinds of things are usually in the background of these paintings and what kinds of things are in the foreground, eg *A painting of people in the outdoors has got trees, fields or mountains in the background and the people are in the foreground.*
- Accept all suggestions at this point, though allow students to disagree with each other if they want to.

1

- Ask students to read the description silently and individually, and then to complete the gaps with the phrases from the box.
- Check answers together when students have finished.

1 in the background	3 in the foreground
2 on the right	4 on the left

2

- Ask students to read the description, decide whether each statement is true or false and to circle 'T' or 'F'.
- Check answers together when students have finished.

1 F 2 T 3 T 4 F

3

- Ask students to read the description again and, this time, match each part of the description with a statement.
- Check answers together when students have finished.

1 d 2 b 3 a 4 c

Language Lab

Aim: to focus on key language skills required to achieve this kind of writing task

- Ask students to read the statements aloud.
- You may ask students to find and underline the examples individually, or to work together as a class.

1 An Airport Scene
2 <u>there's</u> a large bus / <u>there's</u> the airport building / <u>there's</u> a plane / <u>there's</u> a baggage truck / <u>There aren't</u> many people
3 <u>In the foreground</u>, / <u>On the left</u>, / <u>In the background</u>, / <u>On the right</u>,
4 <u>Maybe</u> it's summer. / <u>Perhaps</u> the passengers are

Cool down!

Aim: to personalise what the students have just read

- Ask students to think about other scenes for travelling by plane. Ask them which scene they would like to describe, eg *I would like to describe the scene when the plane takes off. I would like to describe the scene when people meet their friends or family.*
- Encourage them to give reasons and to give a short description of their scene.

HOMEWORK!

Assign exercises 1 and 2 on page 48 of the Workbook.

Plan your project!

Aim: to guide students through the writing process

1

- Explain to students that they are going to write a description similar to the one in the writing section.
- Ask them to look at the picture and answer the questions below. Explain to them that they can answer the questions with a short phrase.
- Check answers together when students have finished.

> Suggested answers:
> 1 a food truck
> 2 a plane
> 3 small planes / airport building / a plane landing
> 4 (part of) an/the airport building

2

- Ask students to look at the picture again and make notes to answer the questions.
- Go over the answers together when students have finished, or go round the class to check students' answers as they complete the notes. Allow students' answers to vary from each other, but point out any inconsistencies that their answers may have in comparison with the photo.

> Suggested answers:
> 1 deliver food to the plane
> 2 large, red
> 3 local business people
> 4 large, plain, made of glass

3

- Explain to students that they are going to complete the *Planner*.
- Point to the first column and explain that these are the different parts of the description.
- Point to the second column and explain that this is useful information about each part.
- Ask the students to write a title and to write as much information as they can (in note form) in the third column.
- Encourage them to use their imagination.
- Check their planners before moving on to exercise 4.

4

- You may wish to assign this for homework or, if there's time, for the students to do it in class.
- Explain to students that they are going to use their notes from the *Planner* in exercise 3 to write their description.
- Explain to them that using their notes is not cheating and that it is important to make a detailed plan before you start writing.
- Allow them to look back at the description in the writing section if they're not sure what to do. At this stage, the most important thing is that the students create a successful piece of writing.
- You may also wish them to consult the *Writing database* on page 136, which has a further model to study.
- You may wish to encourage stronger students to take risks with their writing, but it's probably best if weaker students follow the model completely.
- You may wish to comment on the students' writing before they produce a final version.

> **Additional Tasks and Tests**
> - Student's CD-ROM: Unit 7
> - Teacher's DVD-ROM: Unit 7 Test
> - Teacher's DVD-ROM Test Generator: Unit 7

8

Lucky Escapes!

Target language

Reading skills: reading for gist / specific information (multiple matching, *yes/no* questions)
Vocabulary: topic vocabulary (describing an accident), general basic vocabulary (gestures)
Grammar: past continuous, short answer forms
Listening skills: listening for gist / specific information (multiple matching, multiple choice questions)
Speaking skills: telling simple stories
Pronunciation skills: similar sounding words
Writing skills: story

Get ready!

Aim: to learn and use words and phrases to tell a story

- Ask students to look at the pictures and think about what is happening in each one.
- Ask *Why do you think the photographer took these photos? Have you seen photos like these in an article? What types of articles might have photos like these?*
- You may wish to refer students to the *Vocabulary database* on page 139.
- Give students a short time to match each word or phrase with a picture.
- Review the answers together orally.

1 department store	3 taxi
2 accident	4 autograph

Reading

Aim: to introduce the topic of news reporting

Warm up!

Aim: to introduce the subject of Beyoncé

- Ask students to put their hands up if they have heard of Beyoncé. Write her name on the board if necessary.
- Ask them if they know why she's famous. (She's a singer / pop star.)
- Ask them if they know who she's married to. (Jay-Z)
- Ask them if they know anything else about Beyoncé and Jay-Z. Accept all suggestions, and allow students to disagree with each other if they want to.

1

- Choose a student to read each paragraph of the first article aloud.
- Choose another student to read the second newspaper article aloud.
- Give students a short time to answer the questions about the articles.
- Review the answers together before moving on.

1 A 2 A 3 B

2

- Before students complete the table in exercise 2, ask them to guess which article contains more information, the longer version (Article A) or the shorter version (Article B).
- Give them a short time to complete the exercise by ticking the boxes in the appropriate column.
- Encourage students to underline in the text where they find the answer.
- Review the answers together orally. Ask students if their guess was correct. Ask if they are surprised about which article contains more information.

	Article A	Article B
1	✓	✓
2	✓	
3		✓
4	✓	✓
5		✓
6	✓	✓
7	✓	✓
8		✓
9	✓	
10		✓
11	✓	

2 (…the rapper and hip-hop artist Jay-Z,…)
3 (…successful musician Jay-Z,…)
4 (Article A: She was travelling with her husband,… Article B: … and her husband,…)
5 (…while they were on holiday in London.)
6 (Article A: She asked her driver to stop the car outside *Harrods*,… Article B: The accident happened… …near *Harrods*,…)
7 (Article A: …*Harrods*, the famous London department store. Article B: …*Harrods*, the department store.)
8 (…in Knightsbridge, London, near *Harrods*,…)
9 (Beyoncé and Jay-Z were driving through London to a Japanese restaurant…)
10 (…Beyoncé's Mercedes…)
11 (Beyoncé was extremely lucky.)

3

- Ask students to think about the facts contained in each article. Encourage them to reread the articles if they need to be reminded of the facts as they complete exercise 3.
- Give them a short time to answer the questions with *yes* or *no*.
- Review the answers together orally. Ask students to justify their answers.

1 no
2 no
3 no
4 no (…Beyoncé was upset… …decided not to go shopping,…)
5 yes (…but the couple decided to continue to the restaurant.)
6 no (…they were waiting for a new car to take them…)

4

- Ask students to imagine they are one of the celebrities in the article, Beyoncé or Jay-Z, and tell the story of what happened from that celebrity's point of view.

Cool down!

Aim: to give more practice in telling stories

- Talk about how Beyoncé's experience was both unlucky (because she had a scary experience) and lucky (because she wasn't harmed).
- Ask students if they have ever had an experience similar to Beyoncé's, which was both unlucky and lucky.
- Invite students to tell the class about a time when they were both lucky and unlucky.

Wordpower!

Aim: to develop students' topic vocabulary

- Tell students that all the answers are in the news articles they have read.
- Ask them to try unscrambling the words and phrases to complete each sentence without referring back to the text, but explain that they can if they need to.
- Remind them to be careful with their spelling.
- You may also wish to refer students to the *Vocabulary database* on page 139.
- Check the answers together orally.

1 lucky	5 knocked
2 escape	6 Extremely
3 crash	7 upset
4 get out	8 successful

Additional Task

- Write the following phrase on the board:

ON THE BOARD

LUCKY ESCAPE

- Tell students there are smaller words hidden in the headline.
- Ask them to keep their eyes on the headline as you call out the following words, one at a time: *cape, yes, ape, cap,* etc.
- Pause after each word and allow students to find the word in the headline.
- Tell students there are more hidden words, but their letters are scrambled. Ask students if they can find any, eg *sea, lake, key, pale, sale, easy,* etc.

HOMEWORK!

Assign exercises 1–4 on pages 49 and 50 of the Workbook.

Grammar 1

Past continuous
Aim: to facilitate students' understanding of the functions and usage of the past continuous

Warm up!

Aim: to give practice in the use of the past continuous for giving an eye witness account

- Write the following on the board:

ON THE BOARD

While I was ...

- Ask students to imagine that they saw their favourite celebrity in their neighbourhood.
- Ask them to begin with *While I was ...* and tell the class what the celebrity was doing when they saw them.

Grammar presentation 1

- Go through the grammar presentation with students. Check they understand the two uses of the past continuous: (1) to show that a situation was in progress when another thing happened, and (2) to show that a situation was in progress at a specific time in the past.
- Review the examples of past continuous.
- Explain that there are more examples and additional information on the past continuous in *Grammar database 15* on page 151 at the back of the book.
- Invite students to read through the information in the *Grammar database* on their own.
- Ask them if they have any questions.
- Assign students the Quick check task on page 151.
- Check answers together orally.

Quick check

Circle these correct answers:
1 saw
2 were you doing
3 No, he wasn't.
4 broke
5 were dancing

1

- Give students a short time to complete exercise 1 by matching each sentence with a diagram.
- Check answers together orally.

1 b   2 a

2

- Remind students that *when* is often used to describe a situation that was in progress at a particular time in the past.
- Give students a short time to complete exercise 2 by putting the verbs into the past continuous.
- Check answers together orally.

1 was riding
2 was cutting
3 were playing
4 were you fishing
5 wasn't travelling, was travelling
6 weren't walking

3

- Give students a short time to complete exercise 3 by putting each verb into the correct tense, past simple or past continuous.
- Ask or assign students to read the paragraphs aloud while students check their answers.

1 were enjoying
2 jumped
3 were sailing
4 happened
5 were watching
6 came
7 went
8 was happening/happened
9 were

Cool down!

Aim: to give students additional practice with the past continuous

- Write the following on the board:

ON THE BOARD

While I ...

play run dance study eat

- Ask students to use *While I ...*, the verbs given and the past continuous to tell the class about something that happened to them. If they can't remember anything, they can make something up.
- If time permits, ask them to take turns retelling a fact about one of their fellow students.

HOMEWORK!

Assign exercises 1–4 on pages 50 and 51 of the Workbook.

Wordpower!

Aim: to develop students' topic vocabulary

1

- Ask students to look through the pictures and notice that all of them involve some sort of movement.
- Give them a short time to choose the correct word or phrase for each picture. Say that all the words and phrases identify ways that people move.
- You may also wish to refer students to the *Vocabulary database* on page 139.
- Check answers together orally.

1 nod your head	4 point
2 shake your head	5 shake hands
3 wave	6 kiss

Additional Task

- Ask students to stand and say to them *Let's play Simon Says!*
- Say that you are playing the role of Simon.
- Explain that Simon gives commands that the students should follow, eg *Simon says shake your head. Simon says wave. Simon says point.* etc.
- Students are to obey only the commands that begin with the words *'Simon says'.* If your command does not begin with these words (for example, if you simply say *Jump up and down*), the students should ignore it.
- If there is time, allow students to take turns playing the role of Simon.

2

- Ask students to look at the same pictures again and think of what the people in the pictures might be saying.
- Give them some time to match the pictures with the sentences.
- Check answers together orally.

1 d	3 b	5 c
2 f	4 a	6 e

HOMEWORK!

Assign exercises 1 and 2 on page 52 of the Workbook.

Listening

Aim: to give practice in listening for gist and specific information

Warm up!

Aim: to familiarise students with language used to describe something that happened

- Ask students to look at the pictures in *Wordpower!* exercise 1.
- Ask students to choose one and describe it using one or two sentences and the past continuous.

1

- Explain to students they will be listening to five people talking.
- Ask students to listen for words that describe ways people move.
- Give them a short time to write a word or phrase from *Wordpower!* exercise 1.
- Play the CD track once all the way through. Repeat if necessary.

1 wave	4 nod your head
2 point	5 kiss
3 shake hands	

CD Track 28

2

- Explain to students that they will listen to the recording again.
- Go through the items in the task and ask students to predict what the speakers might talk about.
- Ask students to choose the correct answer, A, B or C, as they listen to the speakers.
- Play the CD track once all the way through. Repeat if necessary.
- Check answers together orally.

1 B (I was walking down the street ... when I saw my friend Ron.)
2 A (...I hit a man who was standing next to me!)
3 A (They shook hands ... he had food all over his hands. The woman's hand was really dirty!)
4 B (My grandpa ... was eating,...)
5 C (...he had a problem with his teeth.)

CD Track 28

3

- Put students into pairs and ask them complete exercise 3 together.
- For question 1, ask students to have a conversation with their partner about which of the five stories they liked best.
- For question 2, ask students to share a personal story that is similar to one of the recorded stories with the class.

Cool down!

Aim: to further personalise what the students have listened to

- Ask students to each decide which of their classmates' stories they liked best.
- Ask students to justify their choices.

HOMEWORK!

Assign exercises 1 and 2 on page 52 of the Workbook.

Speaking

Aim: to give practice in telling simple stories

Warm up!

Aim: to introduce the topic of funny stories

- Tell students about a funny experience someone you know has had, eg adding salt to their coffee instead of sugar.
- Ask students to remember and tell the class something funny that happened to a friend or family member of theirs.

1

- Put students into pairs or allow them to choose their own partners.
- They may wish to mark or underline examples as they go through the questions.
- Give them a short time to answer the questions in exercise 1.
- Check answers together orally.

3 last Sunday
4 Someone knocked on the door.
5 His dad opened the door.
6 The woman who lives next door.
7 They shook hands.
8 that he had food all over his hands
9 The woman's hand was really dirty. They both laughed about it.

2

- Still in pairs, students should tell each other made-up stories using the three prompts shown.
- Go through the *Phrase Bank!* with students and talk about the style of speaking used when telling simple stories.
- Remind them to use the past continuous tense when telling their stories.
- Encourage them to use their imagination to invent the details of the story.
- Go round the class helping students where necessary.

3

- Ask students to think of their own true funny situation.
- Ask them to refer to the prompts in exercise 2 for guidance and write a sentence of their own which summarises their funny situation.

4

- Ask students to tell the class their stories. This time the details of their stories should be true.
- Remind them to use the past continuous tense when telling their stories.
- Give them feedback on how well they used the past continuous tense to tell their stories.

Cool down!

Aim: to further develop students' storytelling, listening and story comprehension skills

- Invite students to retell a story told by one of their classmates.
- For advanced students, encourage them to retell the full story.
- For less advanced students, ask them to tell one detail of a classmate's story.

SoundSpot

Aim: to give practice in listening to and pronouncing words that sound similar to each other

1

- Ask students to read the words for each question. Don't correct any pronunciation errors they may make.
- Play the recording and ask students to circle the words they hear.
- Check answers together orally.

1 fight	3 niece	5 while
2 riding	4 seat	

CD Track 29

2

- Play the recording again and ask students to repeat the words they hear.

CD Track 30

Additional Task

- Explain to students that you will practise pronouncing some other similar sounding words.
- Write the following words on the board:

ON THE BOARD

right hide feed fit feel

- Ask students to read the words aloud. Check and correct their pronunciation if necessary.

Grammar 2

Short answer forms
Aim: to facilitate students' understanding of when and how to use short answer forms

Warm up!

Aim: to give practice responding in short answer form

- Write the following sentences on the board:

ON THE BOARD

Yes, I do. No, I don't.

- Put students into pairs, and ask them to take turns asking and answering questions about each other.
- Explain that questions should be answered using one of the sentences on the board.
- Encourage students to ask questions about their partner's home life, eg *Do you have a brother? Do you have a sister? Do you have a pet? Do you live near school?* etc.

Grammar presentation 2

- Go through the grammar presentation with students.
- Explain that the shortest answer you can give is a simple *yes* or *no*, but we use short answers to be more polite.
- Review the examples with them.
- Explain that there is more information in *Grammar database 16* on page 151 at the back of the book.
- Ask them to read through the information in the *Grammar database* on their own.
- Ask them if they have any questions.
- Assign students the Quick check task on page 151.
- Check answers together orally.

Quick check

Circle these correct answers:
1 No, I haven't.
2 Yes, they were.
3 Yes, I do.
4 No, she wasn't.
5 Yes, she did.

1

- Ask students to look at the cartoon.
- Give students a short time to choose the correct answers based on what is happening in the picture.
- Check answers together orally.

1 Yes, it is.	5 No, he can't.
2 No, he hasn't.	6 Yes, it is.
3 Yes, he is.	7 No, it isn't.
4 Yes, she can.	

2

- Ask students to look at the picture in exercise 2.
- Give students a short time to write short answers to the questions.
- Check answers together orally.

2 it wasn't	5 she was	7 it wasn't
3 he did	6 it wasn't	8 it didn't
4 they did		

3

- Put students in pairs, and ask them to ask and answer questions about the two pictures in exercises 1 and 2.
- Remind them to use the past simple and past continuous.

Cool down!

Aim: to give students additional practice with short answers

- Ask students if they've had an accident in the past. Ask them questions about what happened, eg *Did it happen this year? Were you hurt? Did you trip while you were texting? Did your mobile phone break?* etc.
- Explain to students that they should answer your questions using short answers.

HOMEWORK!

Assign exercises 1–4 on pages 53 and 54 of the Workbook.

Writing

Aim: to develop skills necessary to write a story

Warm up!

Aim: to encourage students to think up ideas to start building an original story

- Write the following questions on the board:

ON THE BOARD

When did you see the alien?
What were you doing at the time?
What did you say?

- Say to students, *You are going to write the beginning of a short story about an alien.*
- Ask them to note down short answers to the three questions on the board.
- Using their notes, ask students to relate the opening of their story.
- Start them off with an example, eg *I saw the alien on Sunday afternoon while I was eating my birthday cake. 'Oh no!' I said, 'Did someone invite an alien to my party?'*

1

- Ask students to read the story. Encourage them to take note of the sentences and phrases at the beginning of the story that describe what was happening, when it was happening, and what the writer was doing at the time.
- Give students a short time to complete the exercise by ticking the statements that are true.
- Check answers together orally.

1 C   2 C

2

- Give students a short time to read the story again and make notes to answer the questions.
- Tell them that notes can be written as words or short phrases.

Suggested answers:
2 his brother (Sam)
3 in the living room
4 playing a dancing game (on the Wii)
5 their dog Bessie
6 Bessie suddenly jumped up and jumped on Sam.
7 Sam fell over, and hit the TV.
8 The TV fell off the table and fell on the floor.
9 He started laughing.
10 because it was so funny
11 Their dad came into the room.
12 He was angry (about the TV).
13 He thought it was funny.

Language Lab

Aim: to focus on key language found in stories

- Check students' understanding of terminology such as 'title' and 'main tense' before beginning the task.
- You may wish students to find and underline the examples individually, or to work together as a class.

1 A Wii Accident
2 … I was in the living room with my brother Sam. … Our dog Bessie was in the room with us. …Bessie suddenly jumped up and jumped on Sam. Sam fell over, and hit the TV. The TV fell off the table and fell on the floor. It was broken! I started laughing because it was so funny. … our dad came into the room. At first, he was angry about the TV but then he thought it was funny, and started laughing too.
3 We were playing a dancing game on the Wii and we were having lots of fun!
4 While Sam was dancing, Bessie suddenly jumped up and jumped on Sam. While I was laughing, and while Sam was lying on the floor, our dad came into the room.

Cool down!

Aim: to facilitate further creative thought in preparation for storytelling

- Ask students to think back to their alien story from the *Warm up!* exercise.
- Give them a short time to create an interesting title for their story.
- Invite them to think creatively about the story, and consider what kind of title might make someone want to read their story.
- Ask them to share their interesting title with the class.

HOMEWORK!

Assign exercises 1 and 2 on page 54 of the Workbook.

Plan your project!

Aim: to guide students through the process of writing a story

1

- Explain to students that they're going to write an original story.
- Ask them to use their imagination and answer the questions to complete the table.
- Explain that they will use this information to begin writing their stories.

2

- Explain to students that they are going to complete the *Planner*.
- Point to the first column and explain that these are the different parts of a story.
- Point to the second column and explain that this is where they will decide on an interesting title as well as the details of the story, eg what happened, who was there, what each person did or said, etc.
- Ask students to write as much detail as they can (in note form) in the third column to help expand on their story.
- Check their planners before moving on to exercise 3.

3

- You may wish to assign this for homework or, if there's time, have the students do it in class.
- Explain to students that they're going to use their notes from the *Planner* in exercise 2 to write their story.
- Explain to them that using their notes is not cheating and that it's important to make a detailed plan before you start writing.
- Invite them to look back at the story in Writing exercise 1 – *A Wii Accident* – to help guide them through the task.
- You may also wish them to consult the *Writing database* on page 137, which has a further model to study.
- Ask students to draw a picture to illustrate their story.
- You may wish to comment on the students' writing before they produce a final version.
- Invite them to read their story to the class.

Additional Tasks and Tests

- Page 157: Units 7–8 Webquest
- Student's CD-ROM: Unit 8
- Teacher's DVD-ROM: Unit 8 Test
- Teacher's DVD-ROM Test Generator: Unit 8

Units 7-8 Revision

You may wish to use this section in any of the following ways with your class:

As a test

- Advise students a few days in advance that they should review the language from Units 7 and 8.
- Before beginning, go through the instructions for each exercise, making sure students understand what is required of them.
- Give students approximately 30 minutes to complete the exercises in test conditions.
- Collect students' books and mark the tests yourself, handing them back the following lesson. Alternatively, go over the answers in the same lesson and ask students to swap books with their partner and mark each other's work.
- The total number of marks for the test is 44 and the following should be taken as a rough guide to students' performance:

39 and over: Brilliant!
33 to 38: Very good!
27 to 32: Good!
21 to 26: Could be better …
20 or under: Should be better …

As homework

- Assign all of the exercises after Units 7 and 8 have been completed.
- Go through the instructions for each exercise when you assign them, making sure students understand what is required of them.
- You may want to ask students to do this section without referring back to the units at all.
- Check answers in class orally, or by writing them on the board.

As classwork

- You may wish to use exercises from this section as supplementary material if you feel that a certain language area needs more work.
- Select the exercises which you feel best suit your students' needs and assign them either as pair work or to be done alone.

1

1 b 3 f 5 d 7 g
2 c 4 h 6 a 8 e

2

1 wood 5 metal
2 glass 6 plastic
3 cotton 7 rubber
4 leather 8 cardboard

3

1 nod 4 point
2 shake 5 kiss
3 wave 6 shake hands

4

1 hair 4 advice
2 ✓ 5 furniture
3 information 6 ✓

5

1 any 3 lot 5 some
2 many 4 no 6 much

6

1 were watching, knocked
2 wasn't listening, asked
3 was Dad cleaning, took
4 was thinking, phoned

7

1 have 3 did 5 do
2 aren't 4 weren't 6 can't

9

Friends and Family!

Target language

Reading skills: reading for gist / specific information (multiple matching, T/F)
Vocabulary: topic vocabulary (getting on with friends and family), general basic vocabulary (feelings)
Grammar: *can* for ability and requests; *could* for requests, *should* for advice; *must* and *have to* for obligation
Listening skills: listening for gist / specific information (multiple choice questions, identifying speakers)
Speaking skills: asking for, giving and refusing permission
Pronunciation skills: *can / can't*
Writing skills: set of household rules

Get ready!

Aim: to learn and use phrases to talk about getting on with friends and family

- Ask students to look at the pictures, then read these sentences and ask students to say which picture matches the sentence: *I can't go out tonight. I have to stay at home.* (3), *My parents are shouting at me! I'm very upset!* (2), *I'm glad you can come to the party!* (1), *My parents don't listen to me.* (3), *Dad, could you take me to Daniel's party on Saturday?* (1), *Michelle doesn't want to be friends any more. What have I done?* (2)
- Accept multiple picture choices at this point, though allow students to disagree with each other if they want to.
- Give students a short time to complete the gaps with the words in the box.
- You may also wish to refer students to the *Vocabulary database* on page 139.
- Check answers together with students.

1 smile	2 cry	3 frown

Reading

Aim: to give practice in reading for gist and specific information

Warm up!

Aim: to introduce the concept of asking for permission

- Write these phrases on the board:

ON THE BOARD

ASK FIRST? JUST DO IT?

- Ask students to look at the two questions on the board.
- Explain to students that you're going to read out phrases (everyday activities) and that they should decide if each activity is something they have to ask their parents about first before doing, or if it's something they can just do.
- Read out the following phrases – one at a time – and ask individual students to say *Ask first!* or *Just do it!* after each phrase: *go to a party, clean your room, do your homework, go to school, go out at night, use your mum's mobile.*
- Accept multiple choices at this point, though allow students to disagree with each other if they want to.

1

- Ask students to silently and individually read the text. Encourage them to ignore all unknown vocabulary at this stage.
- Ask students some very general and simple questions about the text, eg *What kind of text is it?* (a dialogue), *Who are the speakers?* (Phoebe and Lauren), *What is the text about?* (Lauren can't go to Phoebe's party).
- Give students a few minutes to do exercise 1.
- Check answers together with students.

1 P	2 L	3 P	4 P

2

- Encourage students to do this task quickly but carefully (to help develop their scanning skills).
- Ask students to read the text again, decide whether each statement is true or false by circling 'T' or 'F'.
- Encourage students to underline in the text where they find the answer.

- When they have finished, discuss the answers together. Encourage students to justify their answers by giving reasons.

> 1 F (Why are you frowning, Lauren? … I can't go to your party on Saturday, Phoebe.)
> 2 F (I get upset and they get angry. We start shouting and then I cry.)
> 3 T (Try to smile and explain to them how you feel without getting upset.)
> 4 T (They probably worry about you.)
> 5 F (How can I show them I'm old enough and they can trust me?)
> 6 T (Could you ask your dad for me?)

3

- You can ask students to form pairs and ask and answer the questions in this task, or you can ask students to do the task individually and write their answers in their notebooks.
- Alternatively, you can do this task as a class.

Cool down!

Aim: to encourage students to talk about their own lives and personal experiences

- Ask students if they can remember a time when they wanted to go to a party.
- Ask students to remember what their parents said. Ask them other questions, eg *Was it easy to get permission? Did you have to do something to get permission? Did your parents say no in the end? Why? Did you understand why, or were you very angry? What did you do?* etc.

Wordpower!

Aim: to develop students' topic vocabulary

- Explain to students that all the answers appear in the dialogue they have read.
- Ask students to try to complete the gaps without referring back to the text, but explain that they can if necessary.
- Remind students that they should only write one letter in each gap and that the first letter has been given to help them.
- Encourage them to be careful with their spelling.
- You may also wish to refer students to the *Vocabulary database* on page 139.
- Check the answers orally by asking students to read out the sentences.

1 fair	5 get on with
2 let	6 relationship
3 argue	7 grow up
4 permission	8 allow

HOMEWORK!

Assign exercises 1–4 on pages 56 and 57 of the Workbook.

Grammar 1 G

Can* and *could
Aim: to facilitate students' understanding of the functions and usage of *can* and *could*

Warm up!

Aim: to distinguish between talking about present and general ability, asking for and giving permission and making requests

- Write the following words on the board:

ON THE BOARD

ABILITY, PERMISSION, OR REQUEST?

- Explain to students that you're going to read out three short exchanges and you want them to tell you if each exchange shows ability, permission or request (the first pair of sentences shows ability, the second pair shows permission, the third shows request). Read out the exchanges:

Student A: I can dance.
Student B: OK, show me.

Student A: Can I dance here?
Student B: No, you can't right now.

Student A: Can you dance for me?
Student B: I'd love to!

- If you like, ask students to be Student A and Student B and ask them to repeat the short exchanges.

Grammar presentation 1

- Go through the grammar presentation with students. Check they understand when we use *can* and *could* (*can* for talking about present and general ability, asking for and giving permission and making requests; *could* for talking about past ability, asking for permission politely and making polite requests).
- Explain to students that there is more information on *can* and *could* in *Grammar database 17* on page 152 at the back of the book.
- Ask them to read through the information in the *Grammar database* on their own.
- Ask them if they have any questions.
- Ask students to complete the Quick check task on page 152.
- Check answers orally and ask students to justify their answers, eg *1 Yes, you can stay with Molly.* because we use the bare infinitive after *can*.

Quick check

Circle these correct answers:
1 stay
2 Can I go now?
3 drive
4 Yes, you can.
5 can't

1

- Explain to students that they have to write sentences about the pictures using *can/can't* and *could/couldn't* and the words below the pictures.
- Check answers orally and/or by writing them on the board.

2 She could dance yesterday, but now she can't.
3 He could play basketball last Saturday, but now he can't.
4 She couldn't have a picnic this morning, but now she can.

2

- Ask students to look at the words in each of these items and reorder them to make questions.
- Check answers orally and/or by writing them on the board.

2 Could you drive me to the football match?
3 Can I go to the cinema tonight with Ben / with Ben tonight?
4 Can I stay at Lizzie's house tonight?
5 Could you ask Mr Turner to come in?
6 Could Rachel stay here on Friday night?

3

- Ask students to form pairs. Explain that they are going to interview each other.
- Encourage them to ask full questions, eg *Could you swim when you were five?* and to give full answers, eg *Yes, I could.*
- Ask students to look at the table and to put a tick or cross depending on the answer.
- Students should swap roles when one student finishes with their questions.
- When students have finished, ask them to read their partners' responses from the table, eg *George couldn't swim when he was five years old, but he can now.*

Cool down!

Aim: to review the functions and usage of *can* and *could*

- Write the following on the board:

ON THE BOARD

Wanted: Babysitter
work 5 days a week
speak English
drive a car
do some cooking

- Explain to students that this is a job advert for a babysitter (a person to help with someone's baby).
- Ask students to pretend that they are the ones looking for a babysitter and you are responding to the job advert.
- Ask students to ask you questions using *can* about the details of the job, eg *Can you work five days a week? Can you speak English?*
- Encourage students to ask other questions using their own ideas.
- Encourage them to make a polite request using *could*, eg *Could you come to the house today to meet the baby?*

HOMEWORK!

Assign exercises 1–4 on page 58 of the Workbook.

Wordpower!

Aim: to develop students' ability to recognise and use words that describe facial gestures

1

- Ask students to look at the pictures and complete the emotions using the endings from the box.
- Encourage students to make a guess if they're not sure.
- You may also wish to refer students to the *Vocabulary database* on page 139.
- Check the answers orally and/or write answers on the board.

1 angry	3 scared	5 upset
2 confused	4 surprised	6 worried

Additional Task

- Ask students to make facial expressions that match the words in exercise 1, eg *Can you show me an angry face?*

2

- Ask students to read the short dialogues and complete each gap with an appropriate word from exercise 1. Go round the class helping students where necessary.
- Ask or assign students to read the dialogues aloud and ask students to check their answers as they listen.

1 upset/angry	4 surprised
2 angry/upset	5 scared
3 worried	6 confused

HOMEWORK!

Assign exercises 1 and 2 on page 59 of the Workbook.

Listening

Aim: to give practice in listening for gist and specific information

Warm up!

Aim: to practise listening to conversations

- Ask students to look at the task in exercise 1.
- Ask simple questions about the task and elicit responses, eg *Who do you think is going to speak?* (Liam and his parents), *What is the conversation about?* (Liam is asking permission for something.)

1

- Explain to students that they are going to listen to a conversation.
- Go through the items in the task and ask students to predict what the person might say for each thing, eg *Can I go to a party?* for Item 1, *I can study for the test on Sunday.* for Item 2, etc. Accept all reasonable answers at this stage.
- Play the CD track once all the way through. Repeat if necessary.
- Ask students to choose the correct answer, A, B or C, as they listen to the conversation.

1 A (...there's a party at Oscar's house on Saturday. ... Can I go?)
2 C (And I can get ready for the test on Sunday.)
3 B (I couldn't stay at Paul's house last month...)
4 B (It starts at eight. ... 11 o'clock. The party ends then.)

CD Track 31

2

- Explain to students that they will listen to the recording again.
- Ask them to read through the sentences before they listen, and to suggest what the answer to each item might be.
- Play the CD again. Pause when you hear the first correct answer (*Liam*), and ask students to circle it on the page. Check their answers.
- Play the rest of the recording in its entirety and ask students to listen and work independently circling the rest of the answers.
- Check answers together with students. If necessary play the recording again for students to check incorrect answers.

1 Liam (Well, there's a party at Oscar's house on Saturday.)
2 Liam's dad (You've got a lot of homework at the moment,...)
3 Liam's mum (You're still very young, and we worry about you.)
4 Liam (I'm nearly 13!)
5 Liam (It starts at eight.)
6 Liam's dad (OK, but make sure you do your homework first.)

CD Track 31

3

- Ask students to read the sentence in exercise 3, answer the questions and give reasons for their answers.
- You can ask students to form pairs and discuss these questions with each other, or do the task as a class.

Cool down!

Aim: to personalise what the students have listened to

- Ask students to think about something they are allowed to do now that they weren't allowed to do last year, eg *I can go out with friends until 10pm now, but last year I couldn't.*

HOMEWORK!

Assign exercises 1 and 2 on pages 59 and 60 of the Workbook.

Speaking

Aim: to provide practice in asking for, giving and refusing permission

Warm up!

Aim: to introduce students to basic phrases and questions

- Write the following words on the board:

ON THE BOARD

Yes, of course you can.
No, I'm sorry. I'm afraid you can't.

- Ask students to imagine it's a school night. Say the following questions and ask students to say one of the phrases from the board if they think the action is OK or not OK to do on a school night: *Can I watch a DVD tonight?* (Yes...), *Can I call my friend Lisa?* (Yes...), *Can I stay at Helen's house tonight?* (No...), *Can I go to a party at Rob's?* (No...), *Can I watch TV until 4am?* (No...)

1

- Explain to students that they are going to listen to the dialogue in exercise 1.
- Play the CD track once all the way through. Repeat if necessary.
- Then, in pairs, ask students to read the dialogue.
- When they have finished reading the dialogue, they should swap roles.

CD Track 32

2

- Go through the *Phrase Bank!* with students before you ask students to do exercise 2.
- Put students into pairs, or allow them to choose their own partner.
- Explain that they're going to do a role-play.
- Ask one student to pretend they are a teenager and the other student to pretend they are a parent.
- Ask students to use the information in the boxes to form questions and responses, and to use the phrases from the *Phrase Bank!*.
- Encourage them to use their imagination.
- When one student has asked all the questions, they should swap roles.

Cool down!

Aim: to give students additional practice with asking for, giving and refusing permission

- Write the following phrases on the board:

ON THE BOARD

use your computer
borrow some money
use your mobile phone

- In pairs, ask students to make questions asking for permission from their partner to do one of the things on the board, eg *Can I use your computer?* Their partner should give permission, but set a limit, eg *Yes, of course you can, but you can only use it for an hour.*
- If time permits, ask students to swap roles when they've finished.

SoundSpot

Aim: to practise pronouncing *can* and *can't*

1

- Ask students to look at the words *can* and *can't* in exercise 1 and to practise saying both words. Say them along with students if you like.
- Play the recording and ask students to say each word after they hear it on the recording.

CD Track 33

2

- Explain to students that they are going to listen to the sentences in exercise 2 and ask them to circle the word they hear.
- Remind them to listen carefully for the difference between *can* and *can't*.

1 can	2 can't	3 can't	4 can

CD Track 34

3

- Explain to students that they are going to listen to the sentences again.
- Ask students to say the sentences after they hear them on the recording.
- Pause the recording after each sentence if you need to give students more time to say the sentence.

CD Track 34

Additional Task

- Practise a similar task with *could* and *couldn't*.
- Say the following sentences and ask students if they hear *could* or *couldn't*: *Fred could ride a bike when he was 6. Nancy couldn't play basketball last night. Lynn could understand the teacher. Bobby couldn't see the board very well.*

Grammar 2 G

Should, must* and *have to

Aim: to facilitate students' understanding of the functions and usage of *should*, *must* and *have to*

Warm up!

Aim: to consider how we talk about obligation, lack of obligation and giving advice

- Write on the board:

ON THE BOARD

eat every day
eat every hour
eat fruit with every meal
eat only fruit all day

- Explain to students that you are going to read the phrases on the board.
- Ask students to tell you if they think it's important to do this action or not important (*eat every day* – important, *eat every hour* – not important, *eat fruit with every meal* – important, *eat only fruit all day* – not important).
- Explain that things that are important to do are obligations, things that aren't important to do have a lack of obligation, and when we want others to do these things, we give advice.

Grammar presentation 2

- Go through the grammar presentation with students. Check they understand when we use *should, must* and *have to* (*should/shouldn't* to give advice, *must/mustn't/ have to/don't have to* to talk about obligation or lack of obligation).
- Explain to students that they can use either *must* or *have to* in positive statements of obligation. (At this level, it is not sensible or useful to highlight subtle differences between *must* and *have to.*)
- Explain to students that there is more information in *Grammar database 18* on page 152 at the back of the book.
- Ask them to read through the information in the *Grammar database* on their own.
- Ask them if they have any questions.
- Ask students to complete the Quick check task on page 152.
- Check answers orally and ask students to justify their answers, eg *1 You should tell Monica.* because we use the bare infinitive after *should.*

Quick check

Circle these correct answers:
1 tell
2 you don't have to
3 doesn't have to
4 Yes, we do.
5 shouldn't

1

- Ask students to look at the pictures and the table.
- Ask them to write sentences about Anna and Bobby using *must* or *have to* in the correct form.
- Explain that more than one answer may be possible for some of the items.
- When students have finished, check the answers together.

2 Anna must feed / has to feed the goldfish. Bobby doesn't have to feed the goldfish.
3 Anna doesn't have to cook dinner. Bobby doesn't have to cook dinner.
4 Anna doesn't have to empty the bin. Bobby must empty / has to empty the bin.
5 Anna must tidy / has to tidy her room. Bobby must tidy / has to tidy his room.

2

- Ask students to look at the pictures again and write sentences about themselves.
- Go round the classroom assisting students where necessary.
- When students have finished, ask students to read out their sentences.
- You may wish to extend this task by asking students to close their books, and to repeat what they have to/don't have to/etc do.

3

- Ask students to complete the exercise by writing advice on the second line of each item using *should* and *shouldn't* and a phrase from the box.
- When students have finished, check the answers together.
- Assign students to read out the dialogues. Time permitting, repeat with as many students as possible.

1 You should ask your teacher to help you.
2 You shouldn't get upset with them.
3 You should tell her how you feel.
4 You should try to get on with him.

Cool down!

Aim: to review the functions and usage of *must, should* and *have to*

- Ask students to imagine they're in a theatre.
- Ask them to make sentences using *must, should* and *have to* in both affirmative and negative forms about different things that you are obliged or not obliged to do in a theatre, eg *You must be quiet. You mustn't leave your phone on. You should sit in the middle for the best view. You shouldn't sit too close. You have to pay to get in.* etc.
- Encourage students to use their imagination.

HOMEWORK!

Assign exercises 1–4 on pages 60 and 61 of the Workbook.

Writing

Aim: to develop the skills necessary to write a set of rules

Warm up!

Aim: to familiarise students with the concept of rules

- Ask students if they have seen a sign in a museum or a library that tells them what not to do. If they haven't, ask them to imagine what a sign like that would say, eg *You mustn't touch the paintings.*
- Ask students what types of rules people put on signs like these.
- Accept all suggestions at this point, though allow students to disagree with each other if they want to.

1

- Ask students to read the dialogue silently and individually, and then to answer the questions.
- Check answers together when students have finished.

1 No
2 No
3 to write some rules

2

- Ask students to read the set of rules and choose *Yes* or *No* to answer the questions.
- Check answers together when students have finished.
- Additionally, ask students if they have rules like these in their house. Encourage them to say what's similar, eg *I have to tidy my room once a week too.* and what's different, eg *Rick has to feed the dog and the cat every day, but I don't.*

1 Yes	2 No	3 No	4 Yes	5 Yes

Language Lab

Aim: to focus on key language skills required to achieve this kind of writing task

- Ask students to read the statements aloud.
- You may wish students to find and underline the examples individually, or to work together as a class.

1. See the line breaks in the text.
2. We all have to do the washing up on some days. You mustn't forget on your day! / he must empty the bin / Rick and Emily must both tidy their rooms / They have to put their things in the cupboard / Rick has to feed the dog and the cat every day. He must feed them in the morning and in the evening. / Emily has to take the dog for a walk in the evening. / Dad has to do that. / Mum and Dad must knock before going into Rick or Emily's room. They have to wait for permission to go in.
3. When Rick doesn't have to do the washing up, / She doesn't have to do it in the morning.
4. Rick and Emily shouldn't argue. They should try not to get upset. They should try to get on with each other.

Cool down!

Aim: to personalise what the students have just read

- Ask students if they agree with the set of rules in this house.
- Encourage them to give reasons.
- Ask them what rules they think should change and why.

HOMEWORK!

Assign exercises 1 and 2 on page 61 of the Workbook.

Plan your project!

Aim: to guide students through the writing process

1

- Explain to students that they are going to write a set of rules similar to the ones in the writing section.
- Ask them to write the names of the members of their family.

2

- Explain to students that they are going to choose six of the rules in exercise 2 that they will use for their own set of rules.
- Give them two minutes to complete the task before moving on to exercise 3.

3

- Explain to students that they are going to complete the *Planner*.
- Point to the first column and explain that these are the different rules.
- Point to the second column and explain that this is useful information that they should have for each rule.
- Ask students to write as much information as they can (in note form) in the third column.
- Encourage them to use their imagination.
- Check their planners before moving on to exercise 4.

4

- You may wish to assign this for homework or, if there's time, for the students to do this in class.
- Explain to students that they are going to use their notes from the *Planner* in exercise 3 to write their set of rules.
- Explain to them that using their notes is not cheating and that it is important to make a detailed plan before you start writing.
- Allow them to look back at the set of rules in the writing section if they're not sure what to do. At this stage, the most important thing is that the students create a successful piece of writing.
- You may also wish them to consult the *Writing database* on page 137, which has a further model to study.
- You may wish to encourage stronger students to take risks with their writing, but it's probably best if weaker students follow the model completely.
- You may wish to comment on the students' writing before they produce a final version.

Additional Tasks and Tests

- Student's CD-ROM: Unit 9
- Teacher's DVD-ROM: Unit 9 Test
- Teacher's DVD-ROM Test Generator: Unit 9

10

Being the Best!

Target language

Reading skills: reading for gist / specific information (multiple choice questions, sentence completion)
Vocabulary: topic vocabulary, general basic vocabulary (appearance)
Grammar: comparatives, superlatives
Listening skills: listening for gist / specific information (multiple choice questions – pictures, comprehension questions)
Speaking skills: making comparisons
Pronunciation skills: sounds of letter *o*
Writing skills: description (comparing people's appearance)

Get ready!

Aim: to learn and use adjectives to describe animals

- Draw four columns on the board with these headings:

ON THE BOARD

SNAIL ELEPHANT LION SNAKE

- Ask students to look at the adjectives in the *Get ready!* activity and the animals on the board.
- Ask them which adjectives can be used to describe each of the animals.
- Accept any reasonable answers.
- Give students a short time to fill in the gaps with a word from the box; one of the words will be used twice.
- You may wish to refer students to the *Vocabulary database* on page 139.
- Check answers together orally.

1 large, small
2 short, tall
3 long, short
4 fast, quick, slow
5 weak, strong

Reading

Aim: to give practice in reading for gist and specific information in a text about Aesop's Fables

Warm up!

Aim: to introduce the concept of fables

- Ask students if they know what a fable is (a short tale which teaches a moral, often with animals as characters).
- Ask students if they can remember any fables and to share them with the class.
- You may wish to give students a quick example of a fable, eg the story about the hungry fox and the grapes. Summary: *One day a hungry fox saw some grapes hanging from a vine. He jumped and jumped trying to reach them. After many attempts the fox walked away and said, 'I'm sure they taste bad anyway.'* Moral: It's easy to say bad things about what you can't have.

1

- Read the introduction.
- Assign a student to read the first story.
- Lead a class discussion about the moral of the story. Encourage them to guess what the moral might be, but don't confirm a final answer.
- Assign two more students to read the second and third stories.
- Give students a short time to complete exercise 1 by identifying the correct moral for each story.
- Check answers together orally.

1 B 2 C 3 A

2

- Encourage students to do this task quickly but carefully (to help develop their scanning skills).
- Encourage students to underline in the text where they find the answer.
- Give students a short time to answer questions about each story.
- Check answers together orally.

1 a (…the man gets really hot – and takes off his coat.)
2 a (…the North Wind agrees that the Sun is stronger than him.)
3 b (A hare sees a tortoise and thinks 'I'm much faster than him!')
4 b (…he falls asleep. When he wakes up, he discovers that the tortoise is at the finish line.)
5 b (The lion agrees, and lets the mouse go free.)
6 a (He … uses his little teeth to bite the ropes of the net. The lion is free!)

3

- Encourage students to think about the three stories they have read.
- Give them a short time to note down which character they like best and say why.
- If there is time, invite them to read their answers aloud. Encourage them to note the similarities and differences in their answers.

Cool down!

Aim: to give more practice in talking about animals

- Invite students, one by one, to name their favourite animal and to describe it.
- After the first student describes his/her favourite animal, ask the second student to describe his/her favourite animal.
- Continue in this fashion until all students have had a turn.

Wordpower!

Aim: to develop students' topic vocabulary

- Remind students that all the words in the exercise can be found in the Reading text.
- Ask students to try to complete the gaps without referring back to the texts, but explain that they can if necessary.
- Give them a short time to complete the sentences by writing a word in each gap.
- Remind students that they should only write one word in each gap and that the first letter has been given to help them.
- You may wish to refer students to the *Vocabulary database* on page 139.
- Encourage them to be careful with their spelling.
- Check the answers orally by asking students to read out the sentences.

1 competition	5 agrees
2 right	6 certain
3 eventually	7 discovers
4 gives up	8 by mistake

Additional Task

- Write the following sentence on the board:

ON THE BOARD

Look before you leap!

- Ask students if they know or can guess what *to leap* means (to jump).
- Divide students into pairs or groups.
- Ask them to think of a story they know, or make up their own story, that has the moral 'Look before you leap!'.
- Give them a short time to decide on their story and make notes.
- Ask one volunteer from each pair/group to share the story with the class.

HOMEWORK!

Assign exercises 1–3 on pages 62 and 63 of the Workbook.

Grammar 1 G

Comparatives

Aim: to facilitate students' understanding of the functions and usage of comparatives

Warm up!

Aim: to introduce the use of comparatives

- Say to students *We are going to play a game called Bigger, Better.*
- Explain that you will say pairs of items.
- For each pair you call out, students will take turns identifying which item in the pair is bigger and which one is, in their opinion, better, eg, Teacher: *candy, watermelon* Student: *A watermelon is bigger, but candy is better.* or *A watermelon is bigger and better.*
- Say the following word pairs, and add your own ideas if you wish:
puppy, alligator
biscuit, spaghetti
skateboard, bicycle
tennis ball, football
swimming pool, sea
flower, tree
television, cinema
car, aeroplane

Grammar presentation 1

- Go through the grammar presentation with students.
- Explain that comparatives are used to talk about how things are different from other things.
- Check they understand that *than* is placed between two things being compared; *than* is not used when the comparative describes the noun.
- Give students time to read through the information in *Grammar database 19* on page 153 on their own.

- Ask them if they have any questions.
- Assign students the Quick check exercise on page 153.
- Check answers orally and ask students to justify their answers, eg *1 than* because we use *than* between the things being compared.

Quick check

Circle these correct answers:
1 than
2 easier
3 more beautiful
4 more interesting
5 better

1

- Give students a short time to review the sentences in exercise 1 and tick the ones for which the word in bold is correct; if incorrect, students should write the correct word in the gap.
- Review answers together orally.

1 than	3 ✓	5 better
2 bigger	4 shorter	6 happier

2

- Remind students that comparatives can be formed either by adding *-er* to the end of the adjective, or by adding the word *more* in front of three-syllable and some two-syllable adjectives.
- Give them a short time to complete the sentences in exercise 2 by choosing the correct word or phrase.
- Review answers together orally.

1 more difficult	3 more comfortable
2 more pleasant	4 more interesting

3

- You may wish to have students complete this exercise together as a class or independently.
- Give students time to read through the story and put the adjectives into the comparative form.
- If students are working independently, you may wish to go round the room to check they are comfortable with the different forms of comparative adjectives.
- Check answers by assigning students to read the text aloud.

1 easier	5 better
2 more enjoyable	6 larger
3 bigger	7 fatter
4 stronger	

Cool down!

Aim: give students more practice with comparatives

- Write the following words on the board in the format shown:

ON THE BOARD

wolf		hamster
	big	
	quiet	
	wild	
	small	
	loud	
	scary	
	cute	

- Refer students to the words on the board.
- Ask them to use adjectives from the list to compare a lion and a mouse, eg *A wolf is bigger than a mouse* or *A hamster is quieter than a lion.*
- You may wish to invite students to add more adjectives to the list on the board and make more sentences.

HOMEWORK!

Assign exercises 1–4 on pages 63 and 64 of the Workbook.

Wordpower!

Aim: to develop students' topic vocabulary

1

- Tell students that all the words in bold are used to describe people, animals or things.
- Give them a short time to rearrange the letters to find the word opposites.
- You may wish to refer students to the *Vocabulary database* on page 139.
- Check answers together orally.
- For number 1, point out to students that *thin* is sometimes used negatively (ie it's bad/dangerous to be so thin) but *slim* isn't.

1 slim, thin	2 light	3 light, fair

2

- Refer students to the picture and tell them to observe the differences in the two wrestlers.
- Give them a short time to complete the sentences in exercise 2 by using the words from exercise 1 in the comparative form.
- Check answers together orally.

1 fatter, heavier (in either order)
2 slimmer, lighter (in either order)
3 darker
4 lighter

HOMEWORK!

Assign exercises 1 and 2 on page 65 of the Workbook.

Listening

Aim: to give practice in listening for gist and specific information

Warm up!

Aim: to familiarise students with words used to describe people

- Ask simple questions about students in the classroom and elicit responses, eg *Who is wearing a red shirt? How many girls have long hair? Which boys are wearing leather belts?*

1

- Explain to students they will listen to four descriptions of people.
- Ask students to briefly look at the pictures and to note the differences between them.
- Play the CD track.
- Ask students to choose the correct picture for each person described as they listen to the monologues.
- Review answers orally together.

1 a 2 b 3 b 4 b

CD Track 35

2

- Explain to students that they will listen to the recording again.
- Explain to students they will fill in the gaps with words or short phrases.
- Ask them to read through the sentences before they listen, and to predict possible answers.
- Play the CD again. Pause when you hear the first correct answer (*Toby*), and ask students to write it on the page. Check their answers.
- Play the rest of the recording in its entirety and ask students to listen and work independently to write the rest of the answers.
- Check answers together with students. If necessary play the recording again for students to check incorrect answers.

1 Toby (He's taller than me.)
2 fair (He's got short fair hair…)
3 long (Samantha … has got long dark hair.)
4 the speaker (I'm heavier than her…)
5 Uncle Colin (Much heavier than my dad…)
6 short (He's got short hair…)
7 the speaker (I'm tall … but Carrie's short…)
8 the speaker's (I've got fair hair but Carrie's hair is much darker.)

CD Track 35

3

- Ask students to select someone in the class to describe, but not tell anyone who it is.
- Have students take turns describing the person they selected; remind them not to say the person's name.
- Do not allow students to say anything nasty!
- As each student describes their person, all the other students will have to guess who they are talking about.

Additional Task

- Ask students to carry out a similar task to exercise 3, but describing a famous person instead of someone in the class.

Cool down!

Aim: to further personalise what the students have listened to

- Ask students to consider what they looked like when they were in the first year of primary school.
- Invite them to take turns describing the way they look today compared to the way they looked then.
- Encourage them to talk about their size, the way they wore their hair, the way they dressed, whether they wear/wore glasses, etc.

Additional Task

- Put students into pairs, or if appropriate allow them to choose their own partner.
- Explain that they're going to take turns performing two activities – describing and drawing.
- Student A will select a person in the class to describe. As Student A describes the person, Student B will draw a picture of the person being described.
- Once the picture is finished, Student B will have to guess who the person they have just drawn is.
- When they have finished, students switch roles and repeat the task.
- If there is time, invite students to show their drawings to the class and allow all students to guess who is pictured in each.

HOMEWORK!

Assign exercises 1 and 2 on page 65 of the Workbook.

Speaking

Aim: to give practice in comparing the way people look

Warm up!

Aim: to use comparatives to describe the way people look

- Ask students to think of a person who looks similar to them. It can be a friend, a family member or even a celebrity.
- Invite them to take turns describing how this person looks similar to or different from them, eg *I look a lot like my sister, but she is taller and she has darker hair.*

1

- Give students a short time to read the text and answer the questions.
- Check answers together orally.

1 Angelina	4 Angelina and her dad
2 Angelina and her dad	5 Angelina
3 her dad	6 Angelina and her dad

2

- Ask students to think of two family members.
- Give students some time to complete the table by filling in the information about the way the two family members look.

3

- Using the same two family members, students should complete the table by reading the questions and ticking the correct box.
- Remind them that they may tick the third column if the two family members share a description.

4

- Go through the *Phrase Bank!* with students and check they understand how to use words and phrases, eg *than, isn't, They're both* and *They've both got* when making comparisons between two people.
- Invite students to tell the class about their two relatives using the information they gave for exercise 3 and the phrases from the *Phrase Bank!*.

Cool down!

Aim: to give students additional practice with describing people

- Select random pairs of students and invite each pair to the front of the class.
- Stand the students side by side and ask the class to identify the following:
  Who is taller/shorter?
  Who has longer/shorter hair?
  Who has lighter/darker eyes/skin/hair?
- Ask students to answer using complete sentences.
- Continue inviting pairs to the front until all students have had a turn.

SoundSpot

Aim: to give practice in hearing and pronouncing words with the letter *o*

1

- Encourage the students to say the words aloud, but don't correct their pronunciation at this stage.
- Give students a short time to write the words in the appropriate column of the table.
- Play the recording and invite students to make changes to the table as they listen.
- Check answers together orally.

sounds like 'go': both, post, slow, toast
sounds like 'lost': doll, frog, long, strong

CD Track 36

2

- Ask students to listen to the recording again and repeat the words.

CD Track 37

Grammar 2

Superlatives

Aim: to facilitate students' understanding of the functions and usage of superlatives

Warm up!

Aim: to give practice in using superlatives

- Ask students the following questions about family members, and encourage them to give reasons for their answers:
  Who's the tallest person in your family?
  Who is the funniest person in your family?
  Who looks the most like you?
  Who looks the least like you?

Grammar presentation 2

- Go through the grammar presentation with students.
- Check they understand how to use superlatives to talk about one thing in comparison to other things in the same group.
- Explain to students that there is more information in *Grammar database 20* on page 153 at the back of the book.
- Ask them to read through the information in the *Grammar database* on their own.
- Ask them if they have any questions.
- Assign students the Quick check task on page 153.
- Check answers orally and ask students to justify their answers, eg *1 the tallest* because we add *the* before the superlative.

Quick check

Circle these correct answers:
1 the tallest
2 best
3 faster
4 most amazing
5 happiest

1

- Ask students to look at the picture and write the name of a person in each gap to complete the sentences.
- Check answers together orally.

1 Will	2 Phil	3 Bill	4 Will	5 Phil

2

- Remind students that superlatives can be formed either by adding the words *the most* in front of an adjective or by adding *-est* to the end of the adjective.
- Give them a short time to fill in the gaps with the correct word to complete each sentence.
- Check answers together orally.

1 tallest	5 biggest
2 longest	6 best
3 oldest	7 most dangerous
4 fastest	8 most difficult

3

- You may wish to have students complete this exercise together as a class or independently.
- Give students time to read through the story and put the adjectives into the correct form (normal adjective, comparative or superlative).
- If students are working independently, you may wish to go round the room to check they are comfortable with the different forms of adjectives.
- Check answers by assigning students to read different parts of the text aloud.

2 biggest	10 taller
3 long	11 oldest
4 fastest	12 difficult
5 faster	13 best
6 longest	14 better
7 longer	15 most dangerous
8 tallest	16 most difficult
9 tallest	

Cool down!

Aim: to give practice with the use of comparatives and superlatives to describe people

- Ask a student to choose a favourite celebrity (eg actor, musician, athlete, world leader, historical figure) and describe their contributions to society, using the comparative or superlative, eg *Usain Bolt is the fastest man in the world.* or *Einstein was the cleverest person in the world.*

HOMEWORK!

Assign exercises 1–4 on pages 66 and 67 of the Workbook.

Writing

Aim: to develop skills necessary to write a description comparing people's appearance

Warm up!

Aim: to prepare students to write descriptions of people's appearance

- Ask students to choose a partner and describe their partner's appearance as compared to theirs, eg *I have longer hair than John. John has brown eyes, but I have blue eyes.* etc.
- Give students two minutes to write down as many things as they can about their appearances.
- Ask students to share their descriptions. Discuss similarities/differences among students' descriptions.

1

- Ask students to look at the picture and read the description.
- Review the first answer with them, pointing out why the sentence is incorrect and showing how it can be corrected, eg, by crossing out the word *short* and replacing it with the word *tall.*
- Give students a short time to find and correct six more mistakes in the description.
- Check answers together orally.

The Cameron Family

This is a picture of the Cameron family. Mr and Mrs Cameron are in the middle of the picture. Mrs Cameron is quite ~~short~~ and Mr Cameron is quite <u>short</u>. They're both a bit <u>fat</u>. Mrs Cameron's got long <u>fair</u> hair. Mr Cameron's hair is short and dark. Mr Cameron's wearing a grey shirt and black trousers. Mrs Cameron's wearing a <u>blue</u> dress.

Their children, Harry and Chloe, are standing next to them. Chloe's tall. She's taller than Mr Cameron and Harry but she isn't as tall as Mrs Cameron. Mrs Cameron is the tallest person in the family. Harry's <u>taller</u> than his father, but he isn't as tall as Chloe. Both Harry and Chloe are slim. Harry's got <u>short</u> fair hair. Chloe's hair is long and dark. Harry's wearing a t-shirt and jeans. Chloe's wearing a white top and a green skirt.

2

- Ask students to read the description again.
- Give them some time to put the ideas in the order in which they are mentioned in each paragraph.
- Check answers together orally.

the adults

1 d	3 f	5 c
2 b	4 a	6 e

the children

1 d	3 f	5 c
2 b	4 a	6 e

Language Lab

Aim: to focus on words and phrases used to describe people

- Review with students the different ways we use comparatives (eg the use of *not as* + adjective + *as* to talk about things that are different) and superlatives.
- Read each statement aloud and direct students to underline examples in the description.
- You may wish students to find and underline the examples individually, or to work together as a class.
- Check answers together orally.

1
She's taller than Mr Cameron and Harry...
Harry's taller than his father...

2
...she isn't as tall as Mrs Cameron... ...he isn't as tall as Chloe.

3
Mrs Cameron is the tallest person in the family.

4
Mr Cameron's wearing a grey shirt and black trousers. Mrs Cameron's wearing a blue dress. Their children, Harry and Chloe, are standing next to them. Harry's wearing a t-shirt and jeans. Chloe's wearing a white top and a green skirt.

Cool down!

Aim: to personalise what the students have just read

- Ask students to imagine they are part of the Cameron family.
- Ask them to describe themselves in relation to Harry and Chloe, eg *I'm taller than Harry, but I'm not as tall as Chloe. My hair is the longest.* etc.

HOMEWORK!

Assign exercises 1 and 2 on page 67 of the Workbook.

Plan your project!

Aim: to guide students through the process of writing a description of a family photo

1

- Explain to students that they're going to write a description of a family.
- Explain to them that they are going to answer questions about the people pictured in the family photo.
- Encourage them to use their imaginations to think of names for the family.
- When they have decided on names, ask them to fill in the gaps to identify the family members.

2

- Give students a short time to answer questions about the family members.
- Remind them to use comparative and superlative adjectives to describe the family members in relation to each other.
- Remind them to use the names that they created for each of the family members.

1 the dad (students can write his name)
2 short and dark
3 a red t-shirt and black jeans
4 slim
5 a bit fat
6 all of them

3

- Explain to students that they are going to complete the *Planner*.
- Point to the first column and explain that these are the different parts of the description.
- Point to the second column and explain that this is useful information about each part.
- Ask the students to write as much information as they can (in note form) in the third column.
- Encourage them to use their notes from exercises 1 and 2.
- Check their planners before going on to exercise 4.

4

- You may wish to assign this for homework or, if there's time, have the students complete the task in class.
- Explain to students that they're going to use their notes from the *Planner* in exercise 3 to write their description.
- Explain that using their notes is not cheating and that it's important to make a detailed plan before starting to write.
- You may wish them to consult the *Writing database* on page 138, which has a further model to study.
- At this stage, the most important thing is that the students create a successful piece of writing.
- You may wish to encourage stronger students to take risks with their writing, but it's probably best if weaker students follow the model completely.
- You may wish to comment on the students' writing before they produce a final version.

Additional Tasks and Tests

- Page 158: Units 9–10 Song
- Student's CD-ROM: Unit 10
- Teacher's DVD-ROM: Unit 10 Test
- Teacher's DVD-ROM: Term Test 2 (Units 6–10)
- Teacher's DVD-ROM Test Generator: Unit 10

Units 9-10 Revision

You may wish to use this section in any of the following ways with your class.

As a test

- Advise students a few days in advance that they should review the language from Units 9 and 10.
- Before beginning, go through the instructions for each exercise, making sure students understand what is required of them.
- Give students approximately 30 minutes to complete the exercises in test conditions.
- Collect students' books and mark the tests yourself, handing them back the following lesson. Alternatively, go over the answers in the same lesson and ask students to swap books with their partner and mark each other's work.
- The total number of marks for the test is 44 and the following should be taken as a rough guide to students' performance:

39 and over: Brilliant!
33 to 38: Very good!
27 to 32: Good!
21 to 26: Could be better …
20 or under: Should be better …

As homework

- Assign all of the exercises after Units 9 and 10 have been completed.
- Go through the instructions for each exercise as you assign them, making sure students understand what is required of them.
- You may want to ask students to complete this section without referring back to the units at all.
- Check answers in class orally, or by writing them on the board.

As classwork

- You may wish to use exercises from this section as supplementary material when, for example, you feel that a certain language area needs more work.
- Select the exercises which you feel best suit your students' needs, and assign them either as pair work or to be done alone.

1

1 fair
2 let
3 argue
4 gave
5 get
6 relationship
7 grow
8 allow

2

1 short
2 weak
3 slow
4 fat
5 light
6 dark

3

1 confused
2 worried
3 scared
4 surprised
5 upset
6 angry

4

1 can
2 can't
3 have to
4 don't have to
5 shouldn't
6 could
7 mustn't
8 can't
9 have to

5

1 John is taller than me.
2 Sue is shorter than her mum.
3 Sam is older than Mike.
4 Olivia is prettier than Nicole.
5 Paris is more romantic than London.
6 Texas is hotter than Alaska.
7 Tim is worse than me at tennis.

6

1 Jonah is ~~a~~ tallest child in the class. **the**
2 Simone is the ~~younger~~ of all my friends. **youngest**
3 Liam is the ~~funnyest~~ person I know. **funniest**
4 Tokyo is the ~~bigest~~ city in Japan. **biggest**
5 Who's the ~~more~~ important person in your life? **most**
6 Marcus is the ~~baddest~~ dancer I know! **worst**
7 Everest is the ~~most high~~ mountain in the world. **highest**
8 Judy was the most interesting person ~~than~~ at the party.

11

Planning for Tomorrow!

Target language

Reading skills: reading for gist / specific information (multiple matching, multiple choice questions)
Vocabulary: topic vocabulary (planning for the future), general basic vocabulary (quantity)
Grammar: *be going to* for future plans; *will* for future facts
Listening skills: listening for gist / specific information (multiple matching, sequencing information)
Speaking skills: talking about future plans
Pronunciation skills: words and phrases for quantity
Writing skills: informal email (2)

Get ready!

Aim: to learn and use phrases to talk about planning for the future

- Ask students if they can remember the last time someone took a photo of them. Ask students questions, eg *Who took the picture? When was it? Where were you?*
- Ask students to look at the pictures in exercise 1 and to choose the correct phrase to complete each gap.
- Check answers orally and/or write the numbers of the pictures on the board with the correct answer.

1 the distant past
2 the recent past
3 the near future
4 the distant future

Reading

Aim: to give practice in reading for gist and specific information about planning for the future

Warm up!

Aim: to introduce the concept of future plans

- Write the following phrases on the board:

ON THE BOARD

TOMORROW IN 1 WEEK IN 1 MONTH
IN 1 YEAR IN 5 YEARS

- Ask students to think about where they are going to be or what they are going to do for each of the phrases on the board, eg *Tomorrow I am going to be here in class. In one week, I am going to take a test. In one month, I am going to go on holiday. In one year, I am going to go to another school.* etc.

1

- Ask students to silently and individually read the text. Encourage them to ignore all unknown vocabulary at this stage.
- Ask students some very general and simple questions about the text, eg *What kind of text is it?* (future plans), *Who are the writers?* (James Wilson and Libby Burkle), *What is the article about?* (their life and their future plans)
- Give students a few minutes to do exercise 1. Go round the class helping students where necessary.
- Check answers orally and/or write answers on board.

1 J 2 L 3 L 4 J

2

- Encourage students to do this task quickly but carefully (to help develop their scanning skills).
- Tell students they should choose the correct answer, A, B or C, for each item.
- Encourage students to underline in the text where they find the answer.
- When they have finished, discuss the answers together. Encourage students to justify their answers by giving reasons.

1 B (It's hard because you have to remember all your words.)
2 C (Plays in the theatre are fine, but millions of people see you when you're in a film.)
3 C (I started to program them when I was 10.)
4 A (I'm sure it'll be hard work but very interesting.)

3

- You can ask students to form pairs and ask and answer the questions in this task, or you can ask students to do the task individually and write their answers in their notebooks.
- Alternatively, you can do this task as a group.

Cool down!

Aim: to encourage students to talk about their own lives

- Ask students what they think about James' and Libby's future plans. Ask them if this is something they want to do and why, or why not, eg *I want to be an actor like James because this seems like an exciting thing to do. I don't want to be a computer whizz like Libby because I don't like computers.* etc.

Wordpower!

Aim: to develop students' topic vocabulary

- Tell students that all the answers appear in the texts they have read.
- Ask students to try to complete the gaps without referring back to the text, but explain that they can if necessary.
- Remind students that they should only write one letter in each gap and that the first letter has been given to help them.
- Encourage them to be careful with their spelling.
- Check the answers orally by asking students to read out the sentences.
- For item 6, point out that the verb is *to program*, and that the noun is *(computer) program*, and that this shouldn't be confused with the spelling of *(TV) programme*.
- For item 7, you may wish to point out that *app* comes from the word *application*.

1 for sure	4 drama school	7 app
2 guess	5 whizz kid	8 company
3 play	6 program	

HOMEWORK!

Assign exercises 1–4 on pages 69 and 70 of the Workbook.

Grammar 1

be going to

Aim: to facilitate students' understanding of the functions and usage of *be going to*

Warm up!

Aim: to introduce the idea of plans and intentions for the future using *be going to*

- Write the following phrases on the board:

ON THE BOARD

get good marks	*finish school*
go to university	*get a good job*

- Explain to students that they are going to make a future plan using the phrases on the board.
- Starting with the first phrase, ask students to make a sentence with *be going to* and a time phrase such as *this year, in a few years, when I'm older*, etc, eg *I'm going to get good marks this year.*
- Continue with the rest of the phrases.

Grammar presentation 1

- Go through the grammar presentation with students. Check they understand when we use *be going to* (to talk about plans and intentions for the future).
- Explain to students that there is more information on *be going to* in *Grammar database 21* on page 153 at the back of the book.
- Ask them to read through the information in the *Grammar database* on their own.
- Ask them if they have any questions.
- Ask students to complete the Quick check task on page 153.
- Check answers orally and ask students to justify their answers, eg *1 I'm going to visit Russia.* because we use *going* after *I'm*.

Quick check

Circle these correct answers:
1 going
2 aren't
3 to stay
4 isn't going to
5 No, she isn't.

1

- Explain to students that they are going to tick the correct sentences, underline the mistakes in the incorrect sentences and write the correct form in the gaps.
- Remind them that they don't have to rewrite the whole sentence, only the correct form of the incorrect part.
- Check answers orally and/or by writing them on the board.

1 ✓
2 I going to learn everything I can about computers. (am going/'m going)
3 Are they going sell a lot of CDs? (to sell)
4 ✓
5 What are you go to do after the lesson? (going)
6 ✓
7 Alec isn't going go to drama school next year. (to go)
8 Who you going to tell about your idea? (are you going)

2

- Explain to students that they are going to use the words in each of the items to form questions and use the phrases in brackets to answer the questions.
- Check answers orally and/or by writing them on the board.

2 Q: What are you going to do this evening?
A: I'm/I am going to watch TV.
3 Q: What is Tina going to do tomorrow?
A: She's/She is going to study for a test.
4 Q: Who are you and your family going to see this weekend?
A: We're/We are going to see our grandma.
5 Q: Where is Mike going to stay on holiday?
A: He's/He is going to stay in a hotel.
6 Q: What are you going to study at university?
A: I'm/I am going to study computers.

3

- Ask students to read the text and to complete the gaps using one word only in each gap.
- When students have finished, check their answers together. Ask students to read the text aloud.

1 are	3 you	5 are	7 is
2 going	4 to	6 not	8 to

Cool down!

Aim: to review the functions and usage of *be going to*

- Ask students to form pairs and ask and answer each other about what they are going to do that evening, eg *What are you going to do this evening? This evening I'm going to do my homework.*
- Encourage them to ask specific questions, eg *Are you going to read a book this evening?* and to use the negative in their answers if possible, eg *No, I'm not going to read a book this evening. I'm going to play basketball with friends.*

HOMEWORK!

Assign exercises 1–3 on pages 70 and 71 of the Workbook.

Wordpower!

Aim: to develop students' ability to recognise and use words related to quantity

1

- Ask students to look at the drawings and write the correct phrase in the gaps below.
- Encourage students to make a guess if they're not sure.
- You may also wish to refer students to the *Vocabulary database* on page 139.
- Check the answers orally and/or write answers on the board.

2 almost all of	6 a third of
3 most of	7 a quarter of
4 half of	8 none of
5 almost half of	

Additional Task

- Draw a complete circle on the board. Using a marker or a piece of chalk, shade a quarter of the circle and ask students the question *How much of the circle is black* (or blue, or white, depending on what you use)*?* Students should respond *A quarter of the circle is black/blue/white.*
- Then shade more of the circle to illicit *a third of, almost half of, half of, most of, almost all of,* and *all of.* Erase all of the shading to illicit *none of.*

2

- Ask students to read the text and complete each gap with an appropriate quantity phrase from exercise 1. Go round the class helping students where necessary.
- Remind students that the numbers in brackets are there to help them decide which quantity phrase they should use.
- Ask or assign a student or students to read the text aloud and ask students to check their answers as they listen.

1 all of	4 half of
2 almost all of	5 almost half of
3 none of	6 most of

HOMEWORK!

Assign exercises 1 and 2 on page 72 of the Workbook.

Listening

Aim: to give practice in listening for gist and specific information

Warm up!

Aim: to practise listening to conversations

- Ask students to read the rubric and the answers for exercise 1.
- Ask simple questions about the exercise and elicit responses, eg *Who is going to talk?* (three teenagers), *What are they going to talk about?* (The different activities listed in the answers below.)

1

- Explain to students that they are going to listen to three teenagers talking about what they're going to do.
- Explain to students that there is one activity that none of the teenagers will talk about.
- Ask students to match the correct activities with the speakers as they listen to the conversation.

- Play the CD track once all the way through. Repeat if necessary.

Speaker 1 b (We're going to see my grandparents this weekend,…) Speaker 2 a (…I'm going to meet some of my friends…) Speaker 3 d (…I'm going to tidy my room this evening.)

CD Track 38

2

- Explain to students that they will listen to the recording again.
- Ask them to look at the photos and to say what each of these things are (and, if appropriate, what activity they represent) before starting the exercise, eg *The first picture for Speaker 1 is a tennis racket, so the activity is playing tennis.* etc.
- Explain to students that for this exercise, they are going to listen to the recording again and as they listen, they are going to write numbers under the pictures. They will write the number *1* under the picture that shows the first thing that the speaker does, *2* under the second thing and *3* under the third thing.
- Play the CD again. Pause when you hear the first correct answer (*b-1*), and ask students to write *1* under the picture that shows what the speaker does first. Check their answers.
- Play the rest of the recording in its entirety and ask students to listen and work independently to complete the rest of the answers.
- Check answers together with students. If necessary, play the recording again for students to check incorrect answers.

Speaker 1		
a 2	b 1	c 3
Speaker 2		
a 3	b 2	c 1
Speaker 3		
a 1	b 2	c 3

CD Track 38

3

- Ask students to read the questions in exercise 3, answer the questions and give reasons for their answers.
- You can ask students to form pairs and ask and answer these questions with each other, or do the task as a class.

Cool down!

Aim: to personalise what the students have listened to

- Ask students to think about the speakers' plans and say if they've got similar or different plans this week, eg *I'm going to help my mum cook dinner too.* or *Speaker 2 is going to go on holiday this week, but I'm going to go to school.* etc.

- Explain to them that they can look back at the pictures in exercise 2 to remind them of the different activities the speakers are going to do.

HOMEWORK!

Assign exercises 1 and 2 on page 72 and 73 of the Workbook.

Speaking

Aim: to provide practice in talking about plans for the near future

Warm up!

Aim: to introduce students to basic phrases and questions

- Write the following phrases on the board:

ON THE BOARD

go back home   *meet my friends*   *play basketball*
leave my house   *have pizza*

- Explain to students that the phrases on the board are activities for one day during the weekend.
- Ask students to imagine which one of the activities they are going to do first, then put the rest of the activities in order and make sentences using *be going to* and time phrases, eg *This weekend I'm going to leave my house at 12. Then, I'm going to meet my friends at 12.30. Then, we're going to play basketball at one. Then, we're going to have pizza in the afternoon.* etc.
- Allow students to put the activities in the order they wish, and let students argue about the best order.

1

- Ask students to look at the phrases in exercise 1 and tick the things they plan to do in the next seven days.
- Explain to them that if there are any other plans they can think of, they can add them.

2

- Ask students to form pairs.
- Ask students to complete the table by writing the days of the week in the first column and their plans in the second column.
- Explain that they will complete the third column shortly.

3

- Go through the *Phrase Bank!* with students before you ask students to do exercise 3.
- Point out that we use these phrases to talk about future plans.
- You may also wish to refer students to the *Speaking database* on page 144.
- Ask students to use their notes from exercise 2 and the phrases in the *Phrase Bank!*. One student should ask his/her partner about their plans.

- Ask students to write their partner's plans in the third column.
- Explain to them that they can use the model in the exercise to help them.
- When one student finishes asking questions, they should swap roles.

Cool down!

Aim: to give students additional practice in talking about the future

- Ask students to imagine what their parents are going to do during the week and/or at the weekend and talk about their plans, eg *My parents are going to go to work every day this week and this weekend they are going to take me to see my grandparents.* etc.

SoundSpot

Aim: to give practice in pronouncing quantity phrases

1

- Ask students to look at the picture and answer the question, *How many answers did the student get right?* (all of them).
- Ask students to look at the phrases in exercise 1.
- Play the recording and ask students to repeat the sentences as they hear them.
- Encourage them to pay special attention to the weak pronunciation of *of* in each sentence.
- Pause the recording if you need to give students more time to say the sentences.

CD Track 39

2

- Ask a student to read the quotation aloud. If you like, ask all the students to read it aloud at once.
- Explain the word *fool* to students (to make someone believe something that's not true) and then ask students to explain the quotation in their own words, eg *Some people believe everything you say, and sometimes everyone believes one thing you say, but not all people are going to believe you every time.*
- Assist them if they have difficulty explaining the quotation.

Additional Task

- Ask a few students to give you their pencils.
- When you've got the pencils, put half of them in one hand and half in the other.
- Ask students to say how many of the pencils you've got in one hand and how many you've got in the other using quantity phrases, eg *You've got half of the pencils in one hand and half of them in the other.*
- Then split the pencils in a different way, eg some in one hand and most in the other. Ask students to now describe how you've divided the pencils.

- If time permits, continue until you've done all of the quantity phrases.

Grammar 2

will

Aim: to facilitate students' understanding of the functions and usage of *will*

Warm up!

Aim: to introduce the idea of giving and asking for information about future events and facts, and making predictions using *will*

- Write on the board:

ON THE BOARD

Your 3-Day Weather:
Monday: warm with lots of sun
Tuesday: rain
Wednesday: cold

- Explain to students that you're going to ask them about the weather.
- Ask students questions and elicit responses, eg *Will it be warm on Monday?* with a response of *Yes, it will be warm on Monday.*
- Include a question with a negative answer, eg *Will it be warm on Wednesday?* with a response of *No, it won't be warm on Wednesday. It will be cold.*

Grammar presentation 2

- Go through the grammar presentation with students. Check they understand when we use *will* (to give and ask for information about future events and to make predictions).
- Explain to students that there is more information in *Grammar database 22* on page 154 at the back of the book.
- Ask them to read through the information in the *Grammar database* on their own.
- Ask them if they have any questions.
- Ask students to complete the Quick check task on page 154.
- Check answers orally and ask students to justify their answers, eg *1 I'll be famous one day.* because we use *be* after *will.*

Quick check

Circle these correct answers:
1 be
2 won't win
3 They'll be
4 Will you see
5 Yes, she will.

1

- Explain to students that they are going to read the sentences, tick the correct sentences, underline the mistakes in the incorrect ones and write the correct words in the gaps.
- Remind them that they only have to write the incorrect words in the gaps, not rewrite the whole sentence.
- When students have finished, check the answers together.

1 We'll to have a lot of fun at the weekend! (have)
2 Will you are at school tomorrow? (be)
3 Ralph will does well in the future. (do)
4 ✓
5 Does Ben will win the match on Friday? (Will Ben win)
6 ✓

2

- Explain to students that they are going to write sentences and questions by reordering the words in each item, as in the example.
- When students have finished, check the answers together orally.

2 He'll win after so much practice.
3 Jack won't be successful because he's lazy.
4 Will the band be a success?
5 I think she'll love it.
6 It'll be very hot in Spain.
7 I won't enjoy being on a plane.
8 Yes, but it won't be easy.

3

- Ask students to complete the text by writing a verb from the box in each gap using *will* or *won't*.
- Remind students to use short forms where appropriate.
- When students have finished, check the answers together.
- Assign students to read out the text. Time permitting repeat with as many students as possible.

1 will happen	5 Will, make
2 will have	6 will go
3 won't stay	7 will try
4 will work	8 won't spend

4

- Explain what a fortune-teller is (a person who can see the future) and say that the students should imagine they are going to visit one.
- Ask students to think of five questions to ask the fortune-teller.
- Go round the class and check to see if students are using *will* in their questions and writing their questions properly.

5

- Ask students to form pairs.
- Explain to students that they are going to do a role-play.
- Explain to students that one of them is going to be a visitor to a fortune-teller and the other is going to be the fortune-teller. The student who is the visitor will ask their questions from exercise 4 and the student who is the fortune-teller will answer using *will* or *won't*.
- You may want to encourage the students being the fortune-tellers to give reasons for their predictions where appropriate, eg *Yes, you will pass your exams next June because you always do your homework.*
- When students have finished asking their questions, they should swap roles.

Cool down!

Aim: to review the functions and usage of *will*

- Write the following phrases on the board:

ON THE BOARD

Jill loves to sing.
Martin loves to dance.
Lisa doesn't like to write.

- Ask students to make predictions about these three people's futures based on what they like or don't like doing, eg *Jill will be a singer. Martin will be a dancer. Lisa won't be a writer.*

HOMEWORK!

Assign exercises 1–4 on pages 73 and 74 of the Workbook.

Writing

Aim: to further develop the skills necessary to write an informal email

Warm up!

Aim: to develop awareness of appropriate language use in writing an informal email

- Write the following phrases on the board:

ON THE BOARD

Dear Ms Smith	*Hi Fran!*
How are you?	*Thank you for your email.*
See you soon!	*I am looking forward to meeting you.*
Best regards	*Bye for now!*

- Ask students to look at the phrases and explain that as you read each of them, you want students to tell you if we write them in a formal email or an informal email (*Dear Ms Smith*, *Thank you for your email*, *I am looking forward to meeting you*, and *Best regards* are formal; *Hi Fran!*, *How are you?*, *See you soon!*, and *Bye for now!* are informal).
- Ask students if they can think of who you write informal emails to (close friends and family members).

1

- Ask students to read the parts of the email which are in jumbled order.

- Tell them to match the parts of the email with the part numbers listed at the top of the page.
- Check answers together orally when students have finished.

Part 1 h	Part 4 a	Part 7 b
Part 2 d	Part 5 f	Part 8 g
Part 3 c	Part 6 e	

2

- Ask students to read the email again and to choose the correct answers, A or B.
- Encourage them to underline where they found their answers in the email.
- Check answers orally together when students have finished.

> 1 B (Now I have to go to London… And my family are going to come too!)
> 2 B (Now I have to go to London and sing in front of some other people.)

Language Lab

Aim: to focus on key language skills required to achieve this kind of writing task

- Ask students to read the statements aloud.
- Check their understanding of the meaning of 'short forms' before they attempt the task.
- You may wish students to find and underline the examples individually, or to work together as a class.

> 1 Hi Shan!
> 2 I'm in a competition / I'm going to practise / I'm going to learn two songs / I'll choose one of them / I'm not so sure! / I hope everything's OK. / we're going to go out for a meal / It'll be a lot of fun, and it doesn't matter if I win or lose. / It'll be nice / I think they'll be as nervous as me! / We're going to go by train, and we're going to stay in a hotel in London. / It'll be a great day!
> 3 I'm going to practise a lot / I'm going to learn two songs / My music teacher is going to help me. / After the competition, we're going to go out for a meal. / And my family are going to come too! / We're going to go by train, and we're going to stay in a hotel in London.
> 4 I'll choose one of them later / She says I will definitely win. / It'll be a lot of fun, / It'll be nice to have them there / I think they'll be as nervous as me! / It'll be a great day!

Cool down!

Aim: to personalise what the students have just read

- Ask students if they write emails to their friends.
- Ask them to explain what they usually write about. If they don't write emails to their friends, ask them to imagine what they would say in an email, eg *I write to my friend Gary a lot and I usually tell him what's going on in my life.*

HOMEWORK!

Assign exercises 1 and 2 on page 74 of the Workbook.

Plan your project!

Aim: to guide students through the writing process

1

- Explain to students that they are going to write an email similar to Skye's.
- Explain to them that they are going to imagine they are in a competition like *Pop Factor.*
- Ask them to make notes to answer the questions in the task.
- Give them two to three minutes to do this before moving on to exercise 2.

2

- Explain to students that they are going to complete the *Planner*.
- Point to the first column and explain that these are the different parts of the email.
- Point to the second column and explain that this is useful information about each part.
- Ask the students to write as much information as they can (in note form) in the third column.
- Encourage them to use their imagination.
- Check their planners before moving on to exercise 3.

3

- You may wish to assign this for homework or, if there's time, for the students to do the task in class.
- Explain to students that they are going to use their notes from the *Planner* in exercise 2 to write their email.
- Explain to them that using their notes is not cheating and that it is important to make a detailed plan before they start writing.
- Allow them to look back at Skye's email if they're not sure what to do. At this stage, the most important thing is that the students create a successful piece of writing.
- You may also wish them to consult the *Writing database* on page 134 which has a further model to study.
- You may wish to encourage stronger students to take risks with their writing, but it's probably best if weaker students follow the model completely.
- You may wish to comment on the students' writing before they produce a final version.

Additional Tasks and Tests

- Student's CD-ROM: Unit 11
- Teacher's DVD-ROM: Unit 11 Test
- Teacher's DVD-ROM Test Generator: Unit 11

12

Lights! Camera! Action!

Target language

Reading skills:	reading for gist / specific information (matching questions, multiple choice questions)
Vocabulary:	topic vocabulary (film), general basic vocabulary (places)
Grammar:	present continuous for future arrangements, prepositions of time and place
Listening skills:	listening for gist / specific information (multiple matching, T/F)
Speaking skills:	talking about future arrangements
Pronunciation skills:	pronunciation of the word endings *-or, -er, -a*
Writing skills:	interview (dialogue) (2)

Get ready!

Aim: to learn and use words that describe the movie industry

- Ask students to look at the pictures and talk about what they show (people and things that we find on a film set).
- Ask students to label each of the pictures.
- You may wish to refer students to the *Vocabulary database* on page 139.
- Review answers together orally.

1 make-up	3 director	5 camera
2 star	4 costume	

Reading

Aim: to introduce the topic of film extras

Warm up!

Aim: to talk about the difference between stars and extras

- Write the following words and phrases on the board:

ON THE BOARD

Harry Potter movies *The Lord of the Rings*
The Chronicles of Narnia

- Take an informal poll – by asking for a show of hands – of how many students have seen each of the films on the board.
- Ask students who their favourite characters from each film are, eg Harry Potter, Ron Weasley, Hermione Granger. Explain that the main characters are played by actors who are 'stars', eg Daniel Radcliffe, Rupert Grint, Emma Watson.
- Explain that some actors have smaller roles, ie they don't say as many lines.
- Explain that some actors don't say anything at all. They are called 'extras'.

1

- Ask students to silently and individually read the interview. Encourage them to ignore all unknown vocabulary at this stage.
- Ask students some very general and simple questions about the text, eg *What kind of text is it?* (an interview), *Who are the speakers?* (reporter and Ben Lewis), *What is the dialogue about?* (extras in movies)
- Give them a short time to match the questions to the answers.
- Check answers together orally.

1 d	3 a	5 f
2 e	4 c	6 b

2

- Encourage students to do this task quickly but carefully (to help develop their scanning skills).
- Ask students to read the interview again and choose the correct answer to each of the questions.
- Encourage students to underline in the text where they find the answer.
- Check answers together orally.

1 B (…they play the important roles. But there are lots of much less important roles in a film too.)
2 A (…but you can't hear what they are saying.)
3 C (…I've got three different roles.)
4 B (At 12 o'clock we're meeting the director. He'll tell us where to go and where the cameras will be.)
5 B (I do it for fun…)

3

- Ask students to think about the interesting things they learned about the job of a film extra.
- Ask students to express their own opinions about working in film by using the ideas given.
- You may wish to point out that the word *actress* is only used for women, but that these days you can use *actor* for both men and women.
- Ask each student to share his/her opinions with the class.

Cool down!

Aim: to give more practice in talking about films

- Ask students to think about their favourite actor.
- Invite them to take turns telling the class what they like most about this actor.
- Ask them to tell the class what film role their favourite actor is best known for.
- Ask the class to take note of how many of them share the same favourite actor.

Wordpower!

Aim: to develop students' topic vocabulary

- Tell students that all the answers are in the interview they have read.
- Ask them to try filling in the gaps to complete each word without referring back to the text, but explain that they can if they need to.
- You may wish to refer students to the *Vocabulary database* on page 139.
- Remind students they should write only one letter in each gap, and that the first letter has been given to help them.
- Encourage them to be careful with their spelling.
- Check answers orally and/or by writing them on the board.

1 movie	5 action movie
2 roles	6 scene
3 in the background	7 prepare
4 empty	8 shoot

HOMEWORK!

Assign exercises 1–4 on pages 75 and 76 of the Workbook.

Grammar 1 G

Present continuous for future arrangements
Aim: to facilitate students' understanding of how to use the present continuous form to describe future arrangements

Warm up!

Aim: to talk about future arrangements

- Write on the board:

ON THE BOARD

What are you doing after school today?
What are you doing at the weekend?

- Give students an example of how to talk about future arrangements by using the present continuous, eg *I'm going home after school. I'm having dinner with friends at the weekend.* etc.
- Ask students to tell the class what they are doing after school. Then, ask them what they are doing at the weekend.
- Remind them to use present continuous, eg *I'm playing football after school.* not *I will/am going to play football after school.*

Grammar presentation 1

- Go through the grammar presentation with students. Check they understand how we use the present continuous to talk about future arrangements.
- Tell students that they can review the form of the present continuous in *Grammar database 5* on page 147 at the back of the book.
- Ask them if they have questions.
- Ask students to complete the Quick check task in *Grammar database 23* on page 154.
- Check answers together orally before continuing on to the exercises.

Quick check

Circle these correct answers:
1 We're having
2 are you going
3 Are we having
4 I'm not
5 Yes, we are.

1

- Explain that each of the words or phrases in bold is incorrect.
- Give students time to rewrite them correctly.
- Review answers together orally.

1 I'm meeting	4 Who's/Who is
2 making	5 playing
3 Are	6 You're

2

- Explain that the information under the photograph is a schedule used by film extras.
- Ask students to refer to the schedule and answer the questions in exercise 2.
- Review answers together orally.

2 They're trying on the costumes.
3 He's going to the make-up area.
4 She's having a meeting with the director.
5 They're practising the scene.
6 He's/She's filming the scene.
7 They're having lunch.

3

- Explain to students that they will use the same schedule to write questions for exercise 3.
- Check answers together orally.

2 Is Anne having a meeting (with the director)
3 Are they arriving (at the film studio)
4 Is Ben going to the make-up area
5 Are you filming the scene

Cool down!

Aim: to review the use of the present continuous to talk about future arrangements

- Write the following phrases on the board:

ON THE BOARD

having inviting playing eating

- Ask students to talk about what they will do on their birthday.
- Encourage them to use the words on the board, or their own ideas, eg *I'm having a party. I'm inviting all my friends.* etc.

HOMEWORK!

Assign exercises 1–3 on pages 76 and 77 of the Workbook.

Wordpower!

Aim: to develop students' topic vocabulary

1

- Ask students to match the pictures with the words in the box.
- Encourage students to guess if they're not sure.
- You may also wish to refer students to the *Vocabulary database* on page 139.
- Check answers together orally.

1 field	4 beach	6 mountain
2 cliff	5 lake	7 forest
3 desert		

2

- Explain to students that they will use their answers from exercise 1 to complete exercise 2.
- Give them a short time to read the sentences and complete the gaps with the appropriate settings.
- Check answers together orally.

1 field	4 cliff	6 beach
2 desert	5 mountain	7 forest
3 lake		

Additional Task

- Ask students to talk about which of the places they'd choose for different activities, eg *Which place is the best to go camping?* and elicit answers from students such as *The mountains because you can go walking.* or *The beach because you can wake up early and go for a swim.*
- Other possible activities: to go on holiday/have a picnic/ have a party/ watch the stars/play games, etc.

HOMEWORK!

Assign exercises 1 and 2 on page 78 of the Workbook.

Listening

Aim: to give practice in listening for gist and specific information

Warm up!

Aim: to encourage students to think and talk about films

- Ask students to imagine they are film directors.
- Ask them which stars they would cast in their movie.
- Ask them who they would ask to be extras in their movie, eg family members, classmates, teachers, friends, other people they know.

1

- Tell students they will be listening to an actress called Lindsay talking about her next film.
- You may wish to pre-teach *bad guys, chase* and *speedboat* depending on the level of the students.
- Ask students to match each day and place as they listen to the interview based on what Lindsay says.
- Play the CD track once all the way through. Repeat if necessary.
- Check answers together orally.

1 c	3 a	5 f
2 e	4 b	6 d

CD Track 40

2

- Explain to students that they will listen to the recording again.
- Ask them to read through the sentences before they listen, and to predict the answers.
- Ask students to listen and decide if the statements are true (T) or false (F) and to circle the correct letter accordingly.
- Check answers together orally. If necessary, play the recording again for students to check incorrect answers.

1 F (...my friends rescue me with a helicopter.)
2 T (I have a fight with a bad guy... Eventually, I push him off and he falls into the sea.)
3 F (In the end, my friends find me. ... On camels!)
4 F (I have to catch and ride a horse to escape the bad guys.)
5 T (...we're doing a scene where I have to ski down a mountain.)
6 F (...the bad guys fly over me in a small plane...)

CD Track 40

3

- Ask students to give their own opinions by answering the questions about films they've seen.
- You may choose to allow students to ask and answer the questions in pairs or as a group.

Cool down!

Aim: to personalise what the students have listened to

- Ask students to use their imagination and think of their own action scene.
- Ask students to describe their scene to the class.
- Ask them where it takes place if they do not mention the setting in their description.

HOMEWORK!

Assign exercises 1 and 2 on page 78 of the Workbook.

Speaking

Aim: to give practice in talking about future arrangements

Warm up!

Aim: to introduce basic phrases used to make plans for the future

- Write the following phrases on the board:

ON THE BOARD

After class, I'm ....
After dinner, I'm ...
Next month, I'm ...
When I'm 18, I'm ...

- Refer to the phrases on the board. Explain that each phrase takes us a bit further into the future.
- Remind students that the present continuous can be used to talk about future arrangements.
- Say that this is true whether we talk about arrangements five minutes into the future or five years into the future, or any amount of time.
- Ask students to take turns completing the sentences on the board with things they plan to do.

1

- Ask students to look at the posters and ask them if they have seen any of these films.
- Ask students to label each poster according to what type of film it represents.
- Review answers together orally.

1 adventure film/movie
2 comedy
3 romance film/movie
4 cartoon
5 science fiction film/movie

Additional Task

- Ask students to create a movie poster for a movie they would like to make.
- Explain to them that the poster should include pictures of the places where the movie is set and one or two of the lead characters.
- They should be sure to include the movie title and the names of the stars.

2

- Put students into pairs. This time it is best to pair one male student with one female student, if possible.
- Explain that they're going to listen to a dialogue between two teens.
- Play the track once all the way through.
- Ask each student pair to read the dialogue, with one student playing the role of Doug and one playing the role of Fiona.

CD Track 41

3

- Ask students to remain in pairs to talk about cinema plans based on the dialogue prompt.
- Go through the *Phrase Bank!* with students before you ask them to do exercise 3.
- Students should supply their own ideas for each of the underlined parts.
- Go round the room and listen in, helping with pronunciation as needed.
- When they have finished, ask students to swap roles and repeat the exercise.

4

- Ask students to look at the list of activities and to guess what a *limousine* is (a luxury car) and what a *world premiere* is (the first time a film/play/etc is shown).

- Ask students to imagine they are a famous actor and to assign times for each of the activities listed.
- Remind them to refer to the *Phrase Bank!* for examples of words and phrases used to talk about future plans.
- You may also wish to refer students to the *Speaking database* on page 144.
- When students have finished deciding their schedule, ask them to tell the class what they are doing and when.

Cool down!

Aim: to give students additional practice using the present continuous to talk about future arrangements

- Ask students to think of any activities they have arranged for the weekend and note them down on a piece of paper.
- Still in pairs, ask students to ask and answer questions about what their weekend arrangements are.

Additional Task

- Ask students what type (action, romance, comedy, thriller) of films they enjoy most, and why.

SoundSpot

Aim: to give practice in pronouncing words that end in *-or*, *-er* and *-a*

1

- Encourage the students to say the words aloud, but don't correct their pronunciation at this stage.
- Ask students to tick the statement that is true.
- Play the recording and ask students to check their answers as they listen.

a ✓

CD Track 42

2

- Ask students to listen to the recording and repeat the sentences.

CD Track 43

Grammar 2

Prepositions of time and place

Aim: to introduce the usages and functions of prepositions of time and place

Warm up!

Aim: to introduce the use of prepositions of time and place

- Write the following words on the board:

ON THE BOARD

PLACE	
cook food	*kitchen*
books	*schoolbag*
sit	*chair*
TIME	
presents	*birthday*
swim	*summer*
ski	*winter*

- Explain to students that we use prepositions to talk about time and place.
- Ask students to look at the words on the board and ask them the following questions *Where do you cook food? Where do you put your books? Where do you sit?* for *PLACE*, and *When do you get presents? When do you swim? When do you ski?* for *TIME*.
- Give them an example to get them started, eg *I cook food in the kitchen.*

Grammar presentation 2

- Go through the grammar presentation with students. Check they understand when and how we use prepositions of time and place.
- Review prepositions, such as *on, in, to, at, near,* and explain that they are placed before times and places.
- Explain to students that there is more information on prepositions of time and place in *Grammar database 24* on page 154 at the back of the book.
- Ask them to read through the information in the *Grammar database* on their own.
- Ask them if they have any questions.
- Assign students the Quick check task on page 154.
- Check answers together orally and ask students to justify their answers, eg *1 next to* because *next* refers to sequence, not place.

Quick check

Circle these correct answers:
1 next to
2 on
3 in
4 home
5 at home

1

- Give students a short time to choose the correct word for each sentence.
- Check answers together orally.

1 to, in	4 to, near
2 at, on	5 to, on
3 at, in front of	6 on, at

2

- Ask students to write one preposition in each gap to complete the short answers.
- Give them some time to complete the exercise as you go round the room and offer help as needed.
- Check answers together orally.
- You may then wish to ask students to close their books and answer the questions again.

2 At	4 In	6 In
3 At	5 On	7 At

3

- Ask students to write a word in each gap to complete the text.
- Go round the room and offer help as needed.
- Check answers by assigning two students to read out the first and second paragraphs.

1 to	4 in	7 in	10 in	13 on
2 on	5 in	8 on	11 to	14 in
3 in	6 to	9 in	12 on	15 in

Cool down!

Aim: to review the functions and usage of prepositions of time and place

- Ask students the following questions *Where were you born? When do you study? Where do you like to spend your free time? Where do you like to go with friends? When do you go on holiday?*
- Add more questions of your own if you wish.
- Invite students to interview you using the same questions or questions of their own.

HOMEWORK!

Assign exercises 1–4 on pages 79 and 80 of the Workbook.

Writing

Aim: to develop skills necessary to write an interview

Warm up!

Aim: to give students practice with basic interview phrases and questions

- Put students into pairs, or allow them to choose a partner.
- Explain that one student will play the role of a TV reporter, and the other will play the role of his/her favourite actor.
- Give them some time to ask and answer questions before asking them to swap roles and repeat the exercise.
- Tell students they may reply with either long or short answers. Encourage them to have fun and be creative with their questions and answers.

1

- Ask students to read the interview and complete the *Factfile* by writing a word, number or short phrase in each gap.
- Go round the room and offer help as needed.
- Check answers together orally.

Made first film at age: 23/twenty-three
Home: Los Angeles (USA)
Reason for living there: (because) that's where Hollywood is
Favourite director: Luc Besson (maybe)
Favourite film: Star Wars
Starting filming next film: (on) Monday
Name of film: 'Run and Hide'
Type of film: action (movie)
Star of film: Lindsay Beckham
Film in cinemas: in about a year

Language Lab

Aim: to focus on key language skills required to achieve this kind of writing task

- Ask students to read the statements aloud.
- Check students understand what they need to do for each statement.
- You may wish students to find and underline the examples individually, or to work together as a class.

1
We're starting on Monday!
2
In Los Angeles, in the USA.
Because that's where Hollywood is!
'Run and Hide'.
Lindsay Beckham.
In lots of different places!
In about a year.
3
In Los Angeles, in the USA.
In lots of different places!
In about a year.
4
Great! What's it called?
It sounds good! When is the film coming to cinemas?

Cool down!

Aim: to personalise what the students have just read

- Ask students if they enjoy reading celebrity interviews in magazines or on websites.
- Ask them if they enjoy watching celebrity interviews on television.
- Encourage a discussion about the type of questions and answers often included in celebrity interviews. What are some things interviewers and fans want to know?

HOMEWORK!

Assign exercises 1 and 2 on page 80 of the Workbook.

Plan your project!

Aim: to guide students through the process of writing an interview

1

- Explain to students that they're going to write an interview with a famous actor or director for a magazine or website.
- Ask them to decide who they are going to interview.
- Give students a short time to complete the *Factfile* on the person they will interview.
- Tell students they can make up any information they do not know.

2

- Explain to students they are going to complete the *Planner*.
- Point to the first column and explain that this is where they will write the questions they will ask the famous person. Remind students they can reply to an answer before going on to the next question.
- Point to the second column and explain that this is where they'll write down the start of the answers. Remind them this doesn't always need to be a complete sentence.
- Ask the students to write as much information as they can in the third column. Remind them this information should be written in complete sentences.
- Check their planners before moving on to exercise 3.

3

- You may wish to assign this for homework or, if there's time, have the students do this in class.
- Explain to students that they're going to use their notes from the *Planner* in exercise 3 to write their interview.
- Invite them to look back at the interview with director Stephen Speel to help guide them through the exercise.
- You may also wish them to consult the *Writing database* on page 135, which has a further model to study.
- Invite students to find (or draw) a picture of the famous person they wrote about and include it with the interview.
- You may wish to comment on the students' writing before they produce a final version.
- Encourage them to share their interviews with the class when finished.

Additional Tasks and Tests

- Page 158: Units 11–12 Webquest
- Student's CD-ROM: Unit 12
- Teacher's DVD-ROM: Unit 12 Test
- Teacher's DVD-ROM Test Generator: Unit 12

Units 11-12 Revision

You may wish to use this section in any of the following ways with your class:

As a test

- Advise students a few days in advance that they should review the language from Units 11 and 12.
- Before beginning, go through the instructions for each exercise, making sure students understand what is required of them.
- Give students approximately 30 minutes to complete the exercises in test conditions.
- Collect students' books and mark the tests yourself, handing them back the following lesson. Alternatively, go over the answers in the same lesson and ask students to swap books with their partner and mark each other's work.
- The total number of marks for the test is 43 and the following should be taken as a rough guide to students' performance:

38 and over: Brilliant!
32 to 37: Very good!
26 to 31: Good!
20 to 25: Could be better …
19 or under: Should be better …

As homework

- Assign all of the exercises after Units 11 and 12 have been completed.
- Go through the instructions for each exercise when you assign them, making sure students understand what is required of them.
- You may want to ask students to do this section without referring back to the units at all.
- Check answers in class orally, or by writing them on the board.

As classwork

- You may wish to use exercises from this section as supplementary material if you feel that a certain language area needs more work.
- Select the exercises which you feel best suit your students' needs and assign them either as pair work or to be done alone.

1

1 third
2 quarter
3 almost all
4 half
5 all
6 most

2

1 director
2 costume
3 camera
4 drama
5 action
6 make-up
7 role
8 star
9 Movie
10 scene

3

1 lake
2 field
3 beach
4 forest
5 desert
6 mountain

4

1 on
2 in
3 at
4 at
5 of
6 outside
7 next

5

1 to
2 It'll
3 going
4 not
5 you'll
6 are
7 I'm
8 will

6

1 Are you
2 going
3 they're
4 not
5 We're
6 I'm

13

Raising Money!

Target language

Reading skills: reading for gist / specific information (multiple matching, T/F)
Vocabulary: topic vocabulary (raising money), general basic vocabulary (position)
Grammar: present perfect simple (*ever/never*), adverbs of manner
Listening skills: listening for gist / specific information (multiple matching, multiple choice questions)
Speaking skills: talking about activities done in the past, asking and answering questions
Pronunciation skills: pronunciation of the word ending *-ed*
Writing skills: blog post (2)

Get ready!

Aim: to learn and use phrases to talk about raising money

- Ask students to look at the pictures and ask them what the boy is doing in each one. (The boy in the first picture is washing a car. The boy in the second picture is buying groceries. etc.)
- Ask students what is similar about these pictures. (They show a boy doing an activity and there is money in each picture.)
- Give students a short time to choose the correct word from the box to complete each phrase.
- Check answers together orally.

1 make	3 waste
2 spend	4 save

Reading

Aim: to give practice in reading for gist and specific information about raising money for charity

Warm up!

Aim: to encourage students to predict the possible content of the article

- Ask students to read the title and the first few lines of the article and to guess what the article is about. (The article is about people who help others who haven't got a lot of money. etc.)
- Ask students to look at the pictures in the article and to say what the people are doing and why. Encourage them to guess for the third picture. (The first man is riding his bicycle. The girl is cooking food. The second man is sitting in a bathtub with food. They are all doing these things for charity. etc.)
- Ask students if the pictures make them want to read the article. Encourage them to give reasons, eg *I like bicycles so I'm interested in this article. I want to read the article because I want to know why the man is sitting in a bathtub of food.* etc.

1

- Ask students to silently and individually read the article. Encourage them to ignore all unknown vocabulary at this stage.
- Give students a few minutes to do exercise 1. Go round the class helping students where necessary.
- Check answers together orally.

1 G	3 K	5 K
2 L	4 L	6 G

2

- Encourage students to do this task quickly but carefully (to help develop their scanning skills).
- Tell students they should decide whether each question is true or false by circling 'T' or 'F'.
- Encourage students to underline in the text where they find the answer.
- When they have finished, discuss the answers together. Encourage students to justify their answers by giving reasons.

1 F (Jenny isn't a person, though! Jenny is Kevin's bike,...)
2 F (This summer, I'm going to cycle to Moscow.)
3 F (Liz Newman has never worked as a cook,...)
4 T (Mine are tastier and fresher,...)
5 F (I've jumped out of an aeroplane.)
6 F (...I'm going to enter the London Marathon this year.)

3

- You can ask students to form pairs and ask and answer the questions in this task, or you can ask them to do the task individually and write their answers in their notebooks.
- Alternatively, you can do this task as a group.

Cool down!

Aim: to encourage students to consider the concept of charities

- Ask students to imagine that they are helping a charity.
- Explain to them that the charity isn't asking for money, but things.
- Ask students to talk about things they could give to a charity besides money, and who they might be for, eg *You can give cans of food to people who are hungry. You can give clothes to people who haven't got any clothes or haven't got the money to buy clothes. You can take meals to people who are ill.* etc.

Wordpower!

Aim: to develop students' topic vocabulary

- Tell students that all the answers appear in the article they have read.
- Ask students to try to complete the gaps without referring back to the text, but explain that they can if necessary.
- Remind students that they should only write one letter in each gap and that the first letter has been given to help them.
- Encourage them to be careful with their spelling.
- Check the answers orally by asking students to read out the sentences.

1 rich	4 charity	7 marathon
2 poor	5 local	8 enter
3 raise	6 messy	

HOMEWORK!

Assign exercises 1–4 on pages 82 and 83 of the Workbook.

Grammar 1

Present perfect simple (*ever, never*)
Aim: to facilitate students' understanding of the functions and usage of the present perfect simple with *ever* and *never*

Warm up!

Aim: to consider past experiences when the exact time they happened isn't important

- Write the following words on the board:

ON THE BOARD

a hard exam *a long book* *a scary costume*
a trip to Africa

- Ask students to look at the phrases on the board and ask them if they have done these things, eg *Have you ever taken a hard exam?* Encourage students to answer with full sentences, eg *Yes, I have taken a hard exam.* or *No, I have never taken a hard exam.*
- When you have finished with all the phrases, encourage students to ask you questions using the phrases.
- Assist students with the use of *ever* and *never* where necessary.

Grammar presentation 1

- Go through the grammar presentation with students. Check they understand when we use the present perfect simple (to talk about past experiences when the exact time they happened isn't important).
- Explain to students that there is more information on the present perfect simple in *Grammar database 25* on page 154 at the back of the book.
- Ask them to read through the information in the *Grammar database* on their own.
- Ask them if they have any questions.
- Ask students to complete the Quick check task on page 154.
- Check answers orally and ask students to justify their answers, eg *1 I have met Ian before* because we use the past participle of *meet* to form the present perfect simple.

Quick check

Circle these correct answers:
1 met
2 seen
3 never
4 Yes, I have.
5 Have

1

- Explain to students that they will look back at the article on pages 114 and 115 and underline all the examples of the present perfect simple that they can find.
- Check answers orally and/or by writing the examples of the present perfect simple from the article on the board.

Have you ever thought about helping poor people? … what they have done to raise money for a charity.

Kevin Peterson has raised over … which has been with him …

'I've cycled to Turkey and back, and I've been all along … I've also cycled … I've raised a lot, … And she hasn't got lost before!'

Liz Newman has never worked as a cook, but she says she's made over 10,000 cakes!

'I'm sure we've all asked ourselves how …'

Greg Lee has done some crazy things for charity! At the same time, he's raised a lot of money.

'I've sat in a bath of … I've jumped out of an aeroplane. … And I've cut all my hair off … I've never run a marathon, but …

2

- Explain to students that they will read the sentences, tick the correct sentences, underline the mistakes in the incorrect sentences and write the correct form on the line.
- Remind them that they do not have to rewrite the incorrect sentences, only the incorrect parts of the sentences.
- Check answers orally and/or by writing them on the board.

1 ✓
2 We've raise lots of money for our charity. (raised)
3 ✓
4 Are you ever sat in a bath of baked beans? (Have)
5 William haven't jumped out of a plane before. (hasn't)
6 I've wrote an email to the charity for more information. (written)

3

- Ask students to read the sentences and write the verbs in bold in the present perfect simple.
- Remind them that some sentences take the question and negative forms.
- When students have finished, check their answers together.

1 has jumped
2 have given
3 has not run/hasn't run
4 Have, ever seen
5 have never heard/'ve never heard
6 Has, told

4

- Ask students to read the text and use the verbs in the box to complete the gaps using the present perfect simple.
- Remind them that they will use one of the verbs twice.
- When students have finished, check their answers orally together. Ask or assign students to read the text aloud.

1 has been	5 have given
2 has raised	6 has become
3 have been	7 have sold
4 haven't asked	8 has helped

Cool down!

Aim: to review the functions and usage of the present perfect simple

- Ask students to mention activities that they have done for other people, either friends or family members, eg *Have you ever made dinner for your family? Have you ever cleaned your sister's room? Have you ever helped a friend with homework?*
- Encourage them to practise making both complete responses and short answers.

HOMEWORK!

Assign exercises 1–4 on pages 83 and 84 of the Workbook.

Wordpower!

Aim: to develop students' ability to recognise and use prepositions of place

1

- Ask students to look at the drawings and complete the gaps with the correct words or phrases from the box.
- Encourage students to make a guess if they're not sure.
- You may also wish to refer students to the *Vocabulary database* on page 139.
- Check the answers orally and/or write answers on the board.

2 beside	5 on top of
3 below, underneath	6 behind
4 above, over	7 between

Additional Task

- Write these words on the board:

ON THE BOARD

above behind below beside between on top of over underneath

- Ask students to look around the room and make a sentence using the word *above* to talk about where objects are in the room, eg *The clock is above the board.*
- Continue with *behind, below* etc until students have made a sentence or two with each one.

2

- Ask students to look at the picture.
- Ask simple questions about the picture, eg *What is this a picture of?* (a charity event), *What are the people doing in the picture?* (selling cakes, playing games)
- Then ask students to read the text and use a word or phrase from exercise 1 to complete the gaps.
- Explain to them that more than one word may be possible as an answer.

1 Next to/Beside
2 on top of
3 above/over
4 under/below/underneath
5 Between
6 behind

HOMEWORK!

Assign exercises 1 and 2 on page 85 of the Workbook.

Listening

Aim: to give practice in listening for gist and specific information

Warm up!

Aim: to prepare for the main listening tasks

- Ask students to look at the answer choices in exercise 1.
- Ask students if they have ever done these things, eg *Have you ever taken a pet for a walk?*
- Explain to students that they can answer with short answers if they like, eg *Yes, I have.* or *No, I haven't.*

1

- Explain to students that they are going to listen to some friends having a conversation.
- Ask students to look at the answer choices again and predict what one of the speakers might say for each thing, eg *I have taken a pet for a walk.*
- Explain to students that one of the answer choices will not be used.
- Play the CD track once all the way through.
- When students have finished marking their answers, check answers orally.

Speaker 1 e	Speaker 3 a
Speaker 2 c	Speaker 4 b

CD Track 44

2

- Explain to students that they will listen to the recording again.
- Ask them to read through the sentences before they listen.
- Play the CD again. Pause when you hear the first correct answer (*B*), and ask students to circle it on the page. Check their answers.
- Play the rest of the recording in its entirety and ask students to listen and work independently to choose the rest of the answers.
- Check answers together with students. If necessary, play the recording again for students to check incorrect answers.

1 B (Last year we walked a long way, which was very tiring because I don't normally do a lot of exercise.)
2 A (He said his car was dirty and I could wash it for him!)
3 A (Some friends and I decided to raise money…)
4 B (And you ask your relatives and your friends to give you money…)

CD Track 44

3

- You can ask students to form pairs and ask and answer the questions in this task, or you can ask them to do the task individually and write their answers in their notebooks.
- Alternatively, you can do this task as a group.

Cool down!

Aim: to personalise what the students have listened to

- Ask students if they would do the things that the speakers did for charity, eg *Would you go on a long walk, or wash cars? Would you sell something like lemonade? Would you sit in a bathtub of food?* etc.

HOMEWORK!

Assign exercises 1 and 2 on pages 85 and 86 of the Workbook.

Speaking

Aim: to provide practice in talking about things that have happened in the past and asking and answering questions

Warm up!

Aim: to familiarise students with basic phrases and questions

- Ask students about the most exciting thing they have done on a holiday trip.
- Encourage students to repeat the question in sentence form using the present perfect simple, eg *The most exciting thing I have done on a holiday trip is ride the London Eye.*
- Encourage them to say who they were with and when it happened, eg *I went with my family to London last summer*, etc.

1

- Ask students to look at the words and to complete the gaps with the past participle of each of these verbs.
- Then ask students to look back at their answers and tick the past participles that are the same as the past simple for that verb.
- When they have finished, check the answers orally and/or write them on the board.
- Alternatively, ask students to take turns writing the answers on the board.

1 visited ✓	4 raised ✓	7 felt ✓
2 ridden	5 met ✓	8 played ✓
3 eaten	6 won ✓	

2

- Ask students to read the activities in exercise 2 and tick the ones that they have done before.
- You can do the activity with the class by reading out each activity and asking students to raise their hands if they have done that particular activity. You can then ask individual students a more specific question, eg *Which country have you visited?* for *visit another country*, etc.

3

- Go through the *Phrase Bank!* with students before you ask students to do exercise 3.
- Point out that we use these words and phrases to ask and answer questions.
- You may also wish to refer students to the *Speaking database* on page 144.
- Ask students to form pairs and explain to them that they are going to do a role-play.
- Ask them to read the information in the boxes for both Student A and Student B, then ask and answer questions based on the activities from exercise 2.
- When students have finished asking questions, they should swap roles.

Cool down!

Aim: to give students additional practice with asking and answering questions

- Ask students to ask and answer questions about what kinds of transport they have been on, eg *Have you ever travelled by plane? Have you ever been on a train? Have you ever taken a taxi?* etc.

SoundSpot

Aim: to give practice in pronouncing the verb ending *-ed*

1

- Ask students to look at the words and say each of the words aloud, but don't correct their pronunciation or answers at this stage.
- Ask students to write the words that end in a 'd' or 't' sound in the left column of the table and the words that end in an 'id' sound in the right column.
- Play the recording and ask students to check their answers while they listen.

Ends with a 'd' or 't' sound	Ends with an 'id' sound
asked	*wasted*
cycled	decided
helped	suggested
jumped	visited
offered	wanted
played	
raised	
travelled	
worked	

CD Track 45

2

- Play the recording again and ask students to repeat the words they hear.
- You can also make a table on the board and write the words as you hear them from the recording, pausing the recording if necessary.

CD Track 46

Additional Task

- Ask students to think of other verbs that end in *-ed* in the past simple, eg *lived, asked, waited, encouraged, walked.*
- Explain to them that they can look in their books for other words, for example, on the pages before the speaking section.
- Write the verbs on the board and ask students to pronounce them together as a class.
- Alternatively, you can make this a game by asking a student to find a verb with an *-ed* ending and say it correctly. If the student gets it right, the student gets to choose another student to think of another verb and say it.

Grammar 2 G

Adverbs of manner

Aim: to facilitate students' understanding of the functions and usage of adverbs of manner

Warm up!

Aim: to consider how someone does something

- Write the following words and phrases on the board:

ON THE BOARD

How do we do it?
fast *slow*
easy *hard*
good *bad*

- Ask students the following questions and elicit responses: *How do we run a race?* (We run fast.) *How do we walk when we are tired?* (We walk slowly.) *How do we do something that's easy?* (We do it easily.) *How do we try to do something that's hard?* (We try hard.) *How did we do on a test with a high mark?* (We did well.) *How did we do on a test with a low mark?* (We did badly.)
- Encourage students to make guesses and write their responses on the board, but without the mistakes, for example, if students say *We walk slow.* write *We walk slowly.*

Grammar presentation 2

- Go through the grammar presentation with students. Check they understand when we use adverbs of manner (to describe how someone does something).
- Explain to students that there is more information in *Grammar database 26* on page 155 at the back of the book.
- Ask them to read through the information in the *Grammar database* on their own.
- Ask them if they have any questions.
- Ask students to complete the Quick check task on page 155.
- Check answers orally and ask students to justify their answers, eg *1 She talked very quietly.* because we use an adverb (*quietly*) to say how someone does something.

Quick check

Circle these correct answers:
1 quietly
2 fast
3 well
4 easily
5 hard

1

- Ask students to look at the adjectives in exercise 1 and write the adverb for each one.
- Encourage them to make guesses and remind them that sometimes the adjective and adverb forms are the same.
- When students have finished, check the answers together.

1 badly	5 hard	8 quickly
2 fast	6 loudly	9 safely
3 well	7 nervously	10 carefully
4 easily		

2

- Ask students to make sentences by reordering the words in each item.
- Explain to them that in two of the sentences, there are two different ways to write the sentence.
- When students have finished, check the answers together orally.

2 I waited patiently at the start of the race./
I waited at the start of the race patiently.
3 The winner ran very fast.
4 The winner tried hard to win the race.
5 I didn't run very quickly.
6 I was happy when I safely finished the race./
I was happy when I finished the race safely.

3

- Ask students to complete the exercise by forming adverbs with words from the box and putting them into the correct gaps.
- When students have finished, check the answers together.
- Assign students to read the text aloud. Time permitting, repeat with as many students as possible.

1 hard	3 easily	5 safely
2 excitedly	4 slowly	6 loudly

Cool down!

Aim: to review the functions and usage of adverbs of manner

- Write a few (or all) of the following sentences on the board:

ON THE BOARD

She's a careful driver. *He's a quick learner.*
They're patient people. *I'm a happy singer.*
You're a loud talker.

- Ask students to change the sentences so that the adjective is used as an adverb, eg *She drives carefully. He learns quickly. They wait patiently.* etc.

HOMEWORK!

Assign exercises 1–3 on pages 86 and 87 of the Workbook.

Writing

Aim: to develop the skills necessary to write a blog post

Warm up!

Aim: to re-familiarise students with the concept of blog posts

- Ask students if they have read a blog post since Unit 5's lesson on blog posts.
- Ask them questions about the blog post, eg *What was the blog post about? Who wrote it? Did you know the person? Do you read their blog posts often?*
- Ask students what kind of information was in the blog post.
- Ask them if they thought the blog post was good and encourage them to give reasons.

1

- Ask students to read the blog post silently and individually, and then to answer the questions.
- Encourage them to underline in the text where they found their answers.
- Check answers together when students have finished.

> 1 F (I decided to sit in a bath of icy water!)
> 2 F (In the past, I've walked a long way…)
> 3 T (I did it on Saturday, and my dad helped me.)

2

- Ask students to read the blog post again and this time match each part of the blog post with a statement.
- Remind students that there is one statement that they do not need to use.
- Check answers together when students have finished.

> 1 d 2 a 3 c 4 f 5 b

Language Lab

Aim: to focus on key language skills required to achieve this kind of writing task

- Ask students to read the statements aloud.
- You may wish students to find and underline the examples individually, or to work together as a class.

> 1 Raising money!
> 2 I've raised money for charity before. In the past, I've walked a long way and I've cooked cakes and sold them. / Have you ever raised money for charity?
> 3 I decided to do something / I decided to sit in a bath of icy water! / I asked my family / I did it on Saturday, and my dad helped me. / He got an old bath and filled it / he put lots of ice in it! / I got into the bath. It was very cold! I sat there for 30 minutes. Then I had to get out because it was so cold. / I raised over £50, and I felt very happy.
> 4 Slowly and carefully, I got into the bath.

Cool down!

Aim: to personalise what the students have just read

- Ask students what they think about what Ewan did to raise money for charity, eg *Do you think it was a good idea? Would you do something like that?*
- Encourage them to give reasons.
- Ask them if they can think of something strange to do around the house to raise money for charity. Give them some ideas if necessary, eg *eat something strange, or a lot of something, jump around on one foot for 30 minutes, keep your eyes closed during the day for ten hours,* etc.

HOMEWORK!

Assign exercises 1 and 2 on page 87 of the Workbook.

Plan your project!

Aim: to guide students through the writing process

1

- Explain to students that they are going to write a blog post similar to Ewan's.
- Ask them to imagine they have done something to raise money for a charity.
- Ask them to read through the activities in exercise 1 and choose an activity to write about.
- Remind them that if they like, they can choose their own activity and write it on the line next to *other*.
- Give students one or two minutes to choose before moving on to exercise 2.

2

- Ask students to use the activity that they chose in exercise 1 and to write notes to answer the questions.
- Remind them that they can answer in short form.

3

- Explain to students that they are going to complete the *Planner*.
- Point to the first column and explain that these are the different parts of the blog post.
- Point to the second column and explain that this is useful information about each part.
- Ask the students to write as much information as they can (in note form) in the third column.
- Encourage them to use their imagination.
- Check their planners before moving on to exercise 4.

4

- You may wish to assign this for homework or, if there's time, for the students to do it in class.
- Explain to students that they are going to use their notes from the *Planner* in exercise 3 to write their blog post.
- Explain to them that using their notes is not cheating and that it is important to make a detailed plan before you start writing.
- Allow them to look back at Ewan's blog post if they're not sure what to do. At this stage, the most important thing is that the students create a successful piece of writing.
- You may also wish them to consult the *Writing database* on page 135, which has a further model to study.
- You may wish to encourage stronger students to take risks with their writing, but it's probably best if weaker students follow the model completely.
- Encourage the students to add photos or drawings to their blog post to make it look more authentic.
- You may wish to comment on the students' writing before they produce a final version.

Additional Tasks and Tests

- Student's CD-ROM: Unit 13
- Teacher's DVD-ROM: Unit 13 Test
- Teacher's DVD-ROM Test Generator: Unit 13

14

Looking Ahead!

Target language

Reading skills:	reading for gist / specific information (matching pictures and paragraphs, selecting statements)
Vocabulary:	topic vocabulary (predicting the future), general basic vocabulary (directions)
Grammar:	first conditional, adverbs of degree
Listening skills:	listening for gist / specific information (identifying information, drawing a route from information given)
Speaking skills:	talking about future possibilities
Pronunciation skills:	pronunciation of *gh*
Writing skills:	article

Get ready!

Aim: to learn and use phrases related to time

- Ask students to look at the answer choices and ask them some questions about the choices, eg *What are most of these numbers in the answer choices?* (years), *What about 21st?* (a particular day), *In answer choice* b, *how many years between the two numbers are there?* (10), *What about in answer choice* h? (100), *And in answer choice* f? (1000)
- Give students a short time to choose the correct answer.
- You may wish to refer students to the *Vocabulary database* on page 139.
- Check answers together orally.

1 d	3 a	5 b	7 f
2 g	4 e	6 h	8 c

Reading

Aim: to give practice in reading for gist and specific information about predicting the future

Warm up!

Aim: to introduce the concept of articles

- Write these words on the board:

ON THE BOARD

MAGAZINE BOOK

- Say a sentence, and ask students to shout out MAGAZINE or BOOK: *This is where we can read articles.* (magazine), *This has got one long story.* (book), *This has got adverts in it.* (magazine), *The front and back of this is often hard.* (book), *This has got many photographs.* (magazine), *This has sometimes got interviews in it.* (magazine), etc.

1

- Ask students to silently and individually read the text. Encourage them to ignore all unknown vocabulary at this stage.
- Ask students some very general and simple questions about the text, eg *What kind of text is it?* (an article), *Who is the writer?* (a reporter), *What is the text about?* (Kirstie Walker and her predictions about her life)
- Ask students to look at the pictures and say which picture is probably most recent (*c*) and which picture is the distant future (*b* and/or *d*).
- Give students a few minutes to do exercise 1. Go round the class helping students where necessary.
- Check answers together orally.

1 c	3 a	5 b
2 f	4 e	6 d

2

- Encourage students to do this task quickly but carefully (to help develop their scanning skills).
- Tell students they should decide which statements Kirstie is sure of and tick them.
- Encourage students to underline in the text where they find the answer.
- When they have finished, discuss the answers together. Encourage students to justify their answers by giving reasons.

1 ✓ (In a month? … It'll be the summer holidays…)
4 ✓ (If I haven't got a driving licence when I'm eighteen, I'll be upset!)
6 ✓ (Look at what life was like a hundred years ago. It was totally different from now.)

3

- Ask students to form small groups of three, or pairs if appropriate.
- Ask students to take turns asking and answering the questions from the article.

Cool down!

Aim: to encourage students to talk about articles and where they appear

- Ask students where they could read an article like the one in the reading section (a school magazine or kids' magazine).
- Ask them what other kinds of articles they could read in these magazines, eg *You could read about school activities or fun things for kids to do.* etc.

Wordpower!

Aim: to develop students' topic vocabulary

- Tell students that all the answers appear in the article they have read.
- Ask students to try to complete the gaps without referring back to the text, but explain that they can if necessary.
- Remind students that they should only write one letter in each gap and that the first letter has been given to help them.
- Encourage them to be careful with their spelling.
- Check the answers orally by asking students to read out the statements.

1 predictions	5 university
2 apply for	6 technology
3 move	7 universe
4 licence	8 scientist

HOMEWORK!

Assign exercises 1–4 on pages 88 and 89 of the Workbook.

Grammar 1

First conditional

Aim: to facilitate students' understanding of the functions and usage of the first conditional

Warm up!

Aim: to learn how to talk about possible situations in the future and the results of those situations using the first conditional

- Write the following words on the board:

ON THE BOARD

What happens if? study hard don't eat lunch late to school watch a funny movie

- Read a phrase from the board and ask students to imagine what will happen if that phrase is true, eg *You will get good marks.* for *study hard, You will be hungry.* for *don't eat lunch.* etc.
- Write students' answers on the board using a first conditional sentence, eg *If you study hard, you will get good marks.* and repeat the sentences to the class.
- You can ask students to repeat the sentences with you if you wish.

Grammar presentation 1

- Go through the grammar presentation with students. Check they understand when we use the first conditional (to talk about possible situations and their results).
- Explain to students that there is more information on the present simple in *Grammar database 27* on page 155 at the back of the book.
- Ask them to read through the information in the *Grammar database* on their own.
- Ask them if they have any questions.
- Ask students to complete the Quick check task on page 155.
- Check answers orally and ask students to justify their answers, eg *1 If it rains tomorrow, I'll stay home.* because we use the present simple in the *if* clause.

Quick check

Circle these correct answers:
1 rains
2 doesn't
3 won't go
4 isn't
5 's

1

- Explain to students that they have to complete the gaps with the correct form of each verb.
- Check answers orally and/or by writing them on the board.

1 will move	5 will have
2 will go	6 won't study
3 will make	7 won't pass
4 won't be	8 won't get

2

- Explain to students that each of the phrases in bold is incorrect.

- Ask students to write the correct form of each of the phrases in bold on the line.
- Check answers orally and/or by writing them on the board.

1 continues	3 aren't	5 is
2 have	4 isn't	

3

- Ask students to read the sentences in each item carefully, then make a new sentence using the first conditional and both of the sentences.
- When students have finished, check their answers together by asking them to read the sentences aloud.

> 2 If it snows tomorrow, I'll go skiing.
> 3 If my sister buys a new mobile phone, she'll give me her old one.
> 4 If our teacher doesn't come to school tomorrow, we won't have a test.
> 5 If my mum lets me get a dog, I'll call it Lucky.
> 6 If my grandparents visit us this weekend, we'll play cards together.

Cool down!

Aim: to review the functions and usage of the first conditional

- Explain to the class that you're going to play a game.
- Starting with *study hard*, explain to students that you would like one student to make a first conditional sentence with *study hard* like you did in the *Warm up!*, eg *If you study hard, you will get good marks.*
- Then, that student has to choose another student to make another sentence with the second part of the first sentence, eg *If you get good marks, you will go to university. If you go to university, you will get a good job. If you get a good job, you will make money.* etc.
- If they run out of ideas for the first phrase, you can start with another phrase, such as *don't eat lunch*, if time permits.

HOMEWORK!

Assign exercises 1–4 on pages 89 and 90 of the Workbook.

Wordpower!

Aim: to develop students' ability to recognise and use phrases for asking and giving directions

1

- Ask students to match each phrase from the box with a picture.
- Encourage students to make a guess if they're not sure.
- You may also wish to refer students to the *Vocabulary database* on page 139.
- Check the answers together orally.

> 1 turn right
> 2 turn around, turn round, turn back (in any order)
> 3 go straight on, go straight ahead (in either order)
> 4 turn left
> 5 cross the road
> 6 go past

Additional Task

- Ask a student to come to the board and give them something to write with.
- Explain that they will pick a starting point and use the chalk or marker to pretend they are driving in a car somewhere.
- Ask the other students to call out the phrases from exercise 1; the student at the board has to follow the directions.
- Tell the students that if the student's car gets to the edge of the board, it will crash.
- Ask the student to begin driving in any direction they want.
- Feel free to participate in the game, but try to encourage students to call out the directions.

2

- Ask students to read the text and complete each gap with a word from exercise 1.
- Remind students that they will use a word from one of the phrases and not the whole phrase.
- Go round the class helping students where necessary.
- Ask or assign a student or students to read the text aloud and ask students to check their answers as they listen.

1 turn	3 Turn	5 Go	7 go
2 go	4 turn	6 cross	

HOMEWORK!

Assign exercises 1 and 2 on page 91 of the Workbook.

Listening

Aim: to give practice in listening for gist and specific information

Warm up!

Aim: to practise listening to directions

- Ask students if they have ever asked for directions, either to a place around town or a place inside a building.
- Ask them about their experience, eg *What did you say? Who did you talk to? Did they help you?*
- Ask them if anyone has ever asked them for directions. Ask them to tell you what directions they gave. If no one in class has been asked for directions, you can ask them to give you directions to some location in the school, such as the exit.

14 Looking Ahead!

1

- Explain to students that they are going to listen to someone giving directions to someone else.
- Ask students to look at the items in the exercise and predict what the speakers might say for a few of the items, eg *Go straight on Earth Street* for *Earth Street*, *Turn left at the museum* for *museum*, etc.
- Play the CD track once all the way through.
- Ask students to circle the correct options as they listen.
- Repeat the CD track if necessary.

1	Earth Street	6	supermarket
2	Sun Road	7	theatre
3	crossroads	8	traffic lights
4	museum	9	shopping centre
5	Mars Street	10	the Moon

CD Track 47

2

- Explain to students that they will listen to the recording again.
- Ask them to take out a piece of paper and explain that they are going to draw a map and show on the map where the man should go.
- Play the CD track again. Pause when you hear the first place on the map (*This is the corner of Earth Street and Sun Road*) and ask students to draw two streets on their pieces of paper, label them *Earth Street* and *Sun Road* and make a small picture of a man to show where the man is now.
- Play the rest of the recording in its entirety and ask students to continue making their maps and using arrows to show where the man should go.
- Pause the recording if necessary to give students a chance to complete their maps.
- Check answers together with students. If necessary play the recording again for students to check their answers. You can draw a map on the board as well, but only do so when students are checking their answers, to avoid them copying your map.

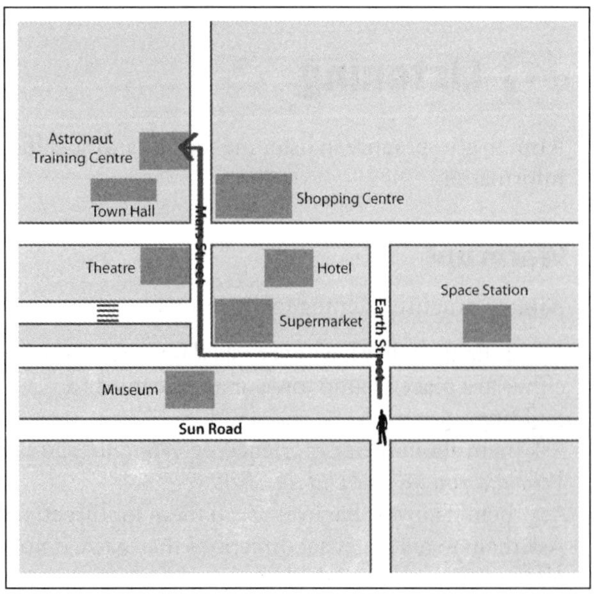

CD Track 47

3

- Explain to students that they are going to do a role-play.
- Ask them to form pairs and pick places on their maps to talk about.
- When students have finished, they should swap roles.

Cool down!

Aim: to personalise what the students have listened to

- Ask students to say how they get from their house to school.
- If you wish, make a map of their directions on the board.

HOMEWORK!

Assign exercises 1 and 2 on page 91 of the Workbook.

Speaking

Aim: to provide practice in talking about future possibilities

Warm up!

Aim: to introduce students to basic phrases

- Ask students to give you some ideas about things to do at the weekend, eg *play a sport, watch TV or a movie, read books*, etc.
- Try to get students to think of as many weekend activities as you can. Assist them with prompts if necessary, eg *What about going to a museum, or the theatre?*
- Ask students if they are going to do any of those things this weekend.

1

- Explain to students that they are going to listen to the dialogue that they can see in exercise 1.
- Play the CD track.
- Then ask students to form pairs and read out the dialogue together.
- When they have finished, they should swap roles.

CD Track 48

2

- Go through the *Phrase Bank!* with students before you ask students to do exercise 2.
- Ask students to remain in pairs and ask each other about their weekend plans.
- Encourage them to give two or three possibilities.
- You may also wish to refer students to the *Speaking database* on page 144.

3

- Explain to students that, for this task, they are going to imagine what their life will be like in two years' time.
- Ask them to make notes on the lines provided.
- Encourage them to use their imagination.

4

- Ask students to tell the class what they imagine their life might be like in two years' time.
- Explain to them that they may use their notes from exercise 3 and phrases they learned from the *Phrase Bank!* for assistance.

Cool down!

Aim: to give students additional practice with talking about future possibilities

- Ask students to think of a famous person and ask them to imagine what that person's life will be like in two years' time, eg *David Beckham will stop playing football in two years. Maybe he will move back to England.*
- Encourage them to use phrases from the *Phrase Bank!* and first conditional sentences, if appropriate.

SoundSpot

Aim: to give practice in the pronunciation of *gh*

1

- Ask students to look at the words and encourage them to say the words aloud, but don't correct their pronunciation at this stage.
- Explain to students that only one of the words contains the letters *gh* pronounced as 'f'. Ask them to listen and circle the correct word.
- Play the recording and then check students' answers.

laugh

CD Track 49

2

- Ask students to listen again, and to repeat the words as they hear them.
- Remind them to be careful of when to pronounce the *gh* like 'f'.

CD Track 50

Additional Task

- Ask students to think of other words that have *gh*. Assist them with the following prompts: *What's the opposite of* day? (night), *What's the past simple of* think? (thought), *What comes after seven?* (eight), *What do we call a trip on an aeroplane?* (flight), *What's the opposite of* low? (high)
- Write the words on the board as students say them.
- Alternatively, you can teach them a couple of new words that have *gh* with the 'f' sound: *cough* and *tough*.

Grammar 2

Adverbs of degree

Aim: to facilitate students' understanding of the functions and usage of adverbs of degree

Warm up!

Aim: to consider how much students like doing something

- Write the following phrases on the board:

ON THE BOARD

reading a book	*playing games*
eating vegetables	*eating pizza*
talking to family members	*talking to friends*

- Say *What do you like doing?* And ask students to use the ideas on the board.
- Ask students to think about how much they like doing the activities on the board.
- Ask if they really like doing one of the activities and encourage them to make a sentence with *really*, eg *I really like eating pizza.*
- Continue practising with *a lot* and *very much*. Remind students that these two phrases go at the end of the sentence.

Grammar presentation 2

- Go through the grammar presentation with students. Check they understand when we use adverbs of degree (to describe the size and quantity of something).
- Explain to students that there is more information in *Grammar database 28* on page 155 at the back of the book.
- Ask them to read through the information in the *Grammar database* on their own.
- Ask them if they have any questions.
- Ask students to complete the Quick check task on page 155.
- Check answers orally and ask students to justify their answers, eg *1 My brother's nearly 18.* because we use *nearly* with a number.

Quick check

Circle these correct answers:
1 nearly
2 difficult
3 quite important
4 very much
5 an extremely

1

- Explain to students that they are going to rewrite each of the sentences in the exercise using the word in bold.
- Ask them to look at the example (item 1) and explain why *a* changes to *an* (because *extremely* starts with a vowel sound).

- Remind them to be very careful with the indefinite article, as they might need to change *a* to *an*, or vice versa.
- Refer them to the grammar box where they can see the position of the adverbs.
- When students have finished, check the answers together.

2 That's a really old computer.
3 That's a very interesting question.
4 You're almost an adult.
5 Driving a flying car is quite difficult.
6 Let's walk really quickly to get there in time.
7 I think about the future a lot.
8 It's nearly time for lunch.

2

- Ask students to read the text and choose the correct word or phrase to complete the sentences.
- When students have finished, check the answers together orally by asking or assigning a student to read the text aloud.

1 a lot	5 an extremely
2 nearly	6 a lot
3 quite important	7 very much
4 really	8 very

3

- Ask students to read the notes in exercise 3 and complete them with their own information using an adverb of degree.
- Go round the class helping students where necessary.
- When students have finished, ask a few students to read out their answers.

Cool down!

Aim: to review the functions and usage of adverbs of degree

- Ask students to think about a competition, such as a race or spelling competition.
- Ask students to say how well you have to do these things to win, eg *You have to run really fast to win a race. You have to be very clever to win a spelling competition. You have to run a lot if you want to be a good runner.* etc.
- Encourage students to use an adverb of degree in their sentences.

HOMEWORK!

Assign exercises 1–4 on pages 92 and 93 of the Workbook.

Writing

Aim: to develop the skills necessary to produce an article

Warm up!

Aim: to get students thinking about the idea of articles

- Ask students if they read magazines.
- Ask them some questions about the magazines, eg *What magazine do you read? Do you read it every day/once a week/once a month? Do you read the whole magazine, or just a few articles? Do you sometimes just look at pictures?*
- If no one in class reads magazines, ask them to talk about magazines in general and imagine what they're like, eg *What kind of magazines are there?* (kids magazines, sport magazines, science magazines), *Where can you get magazines?* (at a book shop or at a corner shop), *Would you like to read a magazine?*
- Accept all suggestions at this point.

1

- Ask students to read the article silently and individually, then answer the questions.
- Check answers together when students have finished.

1 b, c 2 f 3 a 4 d, e

2

- Ask students to read the profile again and, this time, make notes to answer the questions.
- Check answers together when students have finished.

1 food and clothes
2 very happy
3 extremely good
4 It will save people's lives.
5 The children will learn a lot and then grow up and get good jobs.
6 They might help other people.

Language Lab

Aim: to focus on key language skills required to achieve this kind of writing task

- Ask students to read the statements aloud.
- You may wish students to find and underline the examples individually, or to work together as a class.

1 Do you think about being famous? What will you do if you become rich and famous?
2 If I become famous, I'll try to help poor and hungry people in the world.
If I become famous, I'll probably have lots of money! If I have lots of money, I'll give some of it to poor people. … If I do that, it will save people's lives. … But if I do, I'll really try to help other people. … What will you do if you become rich and famous?
3 Maybe I'll also build a hospital. … And perhaps I'll open a school. … Some of them may become famous too! Then they might help other people.
4 very happy, extremely good! will learn a lot … I'll really try to help other people.

Cool down!

Aim: to personalise what the students have just read

- Ask students to imagine they are famous.
- Ask what they will do that's similar to what the writer did (I'll give money to poor people too.) and different (The writer will build a hospital, but I'll build a sports centre.).
- Encourage them to give reasons.

HOMEWORK!

Assign exercises 1 and 2 on page 93 of the Workbook.

Plan your project!

Aim: to guide students through the writing process

1

- Explain to students that they are going to write an article similar to the article from the writing section.
- Explain to them that their article will be called *If I become famous.*
- Ask them to look at the ideas in the exercise and to choose one.
- Encourage them to choose their own idea if they wish, and write it on the line.

2

- Explain to students that they are going to complete the notes in the table.
- Explain that in the first column they are going to write notes about how they and others will feel about them becoming famous.
- Then explain that in the second column they are going to imagine what might happen because of the things they do after they become famous.

3

- Explain to students that they are going to complete the *Planner*.
- Point to the first column and explain that these are the different paragraphs of the article.
- Point to the second column and explain that this is useful information about each part.
- Ask the students to write as much information as they can (in note form) in the third column.
- Encourage them to use their imagination.
- Check their planners before moving on to exercise 4.

4

- You may wish to assign this for homework or, if there's time, for the students to do it in class.
- Explain to students that they are going to use their notes from the *Planner* in exercise 3 to write their article.
- Explain to them that using their notes is not cheating and that it is important to make a detailed plan before you start writing.
- Allow them to look back at the article from the writing section if they're not sure what to do. At this stage, the most important thing is that the students create a successful piece of writing.
- You may also wish them to consult the *Writing database* on page 138, which has a further model to study.
- You may wish to encourage stronger students to take risks with their writing, but it's probably best if weaker students follow the model completely.
- You may wish to comment on the students' writing before they produce a final version.

Additional Tasks and Tests

- Page 159: Units 13–14 Song
- Page 159: Units 1–14 Webquest
- Student's CD-ROM: Unit 14
- Teacher's DVD-ROM: Unit 14 Test
- Teacher's DVD-ROM: Term Test 3 (Units 11–14)
- Teacher's DVD-ROM: Final Test (Units 1–14)
- Teacher's DVD-ROM Test Generator: Unit 14

Units 13-14 Revision

You may wish to use this section in any of the following ways with your class:

As a test

- Advise students a few days in advance that they should review the language from Units 13 and 14.
- Before beginning, go through the instructions for each exercise, making sure students understand what is required of them.
- Give students approximately 30 minutes to complete the exercises in test conditions.
- Collect students' books and mark the tests yourself, handing them back the following lesson. Alternatively, go over the answers in the same lesson and ask students to swap books with their partner and mark each other's work.
- The total number of marks for the test is 41 and the following should be taken as a rough guide to students' performance:

37 and over: Brilliant!
34 to 36: Very good!
29 to 33: Good!
22 to 28: Could be better …
21 or under: Should be better …

As homework

- Assign all of the exercises after Units 13 and 14 have been completed.
- Go through the instructions for each exercise as you assign them, making sure students understand what is required of them.
- You may want to ask students to complete this section without referring back to the units at all.
- Check answers in class orally, or by writing them on the board.

As classwork

- You may wish to use exercises from this section as supplementary material if you feel that a certain language area needs more work.
- Select the exercises which you feel best suit your students' needs and assign them either as pairwork or to be done alone.

1

1 spend
2 rich
3 wasted
4 raise
5 charity
6 saving
7 poor
8 make

2

To get to the river, go down this road to the end. Then, <u>return</u> (turn) left. Go straight on for 100 metres, then <u>turn to</u> (turn) right. Go <u>passed</u> (past) the fire station, and <u>cross to</u> (cross) the road. You'll see a cinema. Turn right again and go straight <u>head</u> (ahead) for 50 metres. The river is there.

3

1 behind
2 on top
3 above
4 beside
5 between
6 below

4

1 If I pass my exam, I will have a party.
2 If you forget your homework, the teacher will be angry.
3 If you tell me your secret, I won't tell anyone.
4 If Victor doesn't study harder, he will fail the test.
5 If you call your parents, they won't worry about you.
6 If it doesn't rain on Saturday, we'll have a picnic.

5

1 Have you ever visited
2 I've travelled
3 have stayed
4 haven't stayed
5 Have you ever had
6 have been
7 have never complained
8 have had

6

1 I was extremely pleased to see Michael.
2 I am really sorry about your dog.
3 He cleans his bedroom very quickly.
4 Darren is nearly as tall as his dad.
5 You nearly hit me with your bag.
6 We passed our exams easily.
7 I/She waited for an extremely long time before she/I arrived.
8 He can solve really difficult maths problems fast.

Answer Key for Songs and Webquests

Units 1–2: Song

1 town
2 never
3 chicks
4 pony
5 nephew
6 great-grandmother
7 puppies
8 second
9 only

Units 3–4: Webquest

1 mall
2 toys
3 Compact Disc
4 Australia
5 Mexico
6 Eton
7 the USA
8 California
9 9th June
10 *Harry Potter and the Philosopher's Stone*

Units 5–6: Song

1 ferry
2 plane
3 carriage
4 ticket
5 Europe
6 South
7 people

Units 7–8: Webquest

1 Gatwick
2 visa
3 aluminum
4 1981
5 December
6 Eleftherios Venizelos
7 glider
8 aeroplane
9 1935
10 taxi

Units 9 –10: Song

1 growing
2 scared
3 frown
4 mistake
5 mistake
6 strong
7 permission
8 weak
9 confused
10 confused

Units 11–12: Webquest

1 Apple Inc.
2 Microsoft
3 Saturn
4 Kentucky
5 2004
6 Jurassic Park
7 1981
8 Asia
9 K2
10 Dover

Units 13–14: Song

1 poor
2 been
3 money
4 made
5 sunny
6 laughed

Units 1–14: End-of-year Webquest

1 Bombay
2 bull
3 six/6
4 Sir Tim Berners-Lee
5 1931
6 reptiles
7 Wright
8 1799
9 dishwasher
10 oxen
11 15
12 1967
13 November
14 Neil Armstrong

Audioscripts

Unit 1

Listening 1 & 2

Interviewer: Hi! And welcome to Street Talk. Every week, we ask people in the street questions and get their opinions. This week, we're talking about people and their families! So let's stop a few people and see what they think. Excuse me. Can I ask you a few questions? What's your name?
Paula: Paula.
Interviewer: And do you have a large family?
Paula: Well, I'm an only child, so not really. I've got four cousins, and two aunts and two uncles. We're very close, but there aren't very many of us!
Interviewer: Do you have any pets?
Paula: I love animals, and my favourite animals are cats. But my dad doesn't like them, so we don't have one. I want one, though!
Interviewer: What's your room like at home?
Paula: It's quite big, and all my things are in there. I've got a lot of books and CDs, and I have pictures on the walls. Erm … I don't have a TV in there, but I've got a computer. I do my homework on it sometimes and I play games.
Interviewer: Thank you! Excuse me. Can I ask you a few questions? What's your name?
Seb: Seb.
Interviewer: And do you have a large family?
Seb: Well, there's me, my brother and my sisters – there are three of them. And my four grandparents and two great-grandparents. I'm very lucky. And there are aunts and uncles and some cousins. We don't all live together, of course!
Interviewer: Do you have any pets?
Seb: There isn't a lot of space in our house for large pets like cats or dogs, so we can't have them. We've got a couple of fish, though, and I like watching them swim around.
Interviewer: What's your room like at home?
Seb: I share with my brother. I've got a small bed and I've got all my things in my half of the room. I don't have a lot of things, but I've got a few books and my laptop. I don't spend a lot of time there. I just sleep there, really.
Interviewer: Thank you! Excuse me. Can I ask you a few questions? What's your name?
Sienna: Sienna.
Interviewer: And do you have a large family?
Sienna: There's me and my brother. My mum and dad don't have any brothers or sisters, so I don't have aunts or uncles. I've got two grandparents and one of them lives with us. That's it, really.
Interviewer: Do you have any pets?
Sienna: I think it's important to have pets because they're part of your family and they can be your friend. I love our dog, Prince. We don't have a cat or anything else.
Interviewer: What's your room like at home?
Sienna: It's beautiful! It's large, and it's full of my things. I've got a wardrobe with all my clothes in – I've got a lot of clothes! And I have a TV and a computer in there. I spend a lot of my time on the internet, talking to my best friend. Oh, and I have about a hundred teddy bears and dolls, and they're all in my room!
Interviewer: Thank you!

Grammar 2, Exercise 3

David: Give it back! It's mine.
Daisy: No, it isn't! It's my t-shirt!
Mum: Hey, you two! What's the problem?
Daisy: David says this t-shirt is his, but it isn't. It's mine!
David: It isn't hers! She gave it to me!
Mum: Well, Daisy, that means it's David's t-shirt, not yours.
Daisy: I only gave it to him because he did my homework for me!
Mum: Daisy! That's very wrong! But it's still his t-shirt.
Daisy: But our teacher gave me an F for that homework!

Unit 2

Listening 1 & 2

Speaker 1
My mum and dad get up really early – at about five o'clock in the morning. That's because they start work on the farm at half past five. The first thing they do is milk the cows. Then they feed all the other animals. I don't help on the farm because I'm still at school so I don't get up so early – thankfully! I usually get up at about half past seven during the week, and nine o'clock on Saturdays and Sundays.

Speaker 2
Yes, it is a difficult job, but I really love it. Mr and Mrs Collins are so nice, and of course it's great working with animals. I don't really like getting up so early – I usually get up at quarter to five! – but it's actually not that bad. I'm usually very tired at the end of the day though, so I sleep well!

Speaker 3
I love living and working on a farm, but it's sometimes difficult, I think, for our daughter Susan. We don't take many holidays because of the animals, and we usually work seven days a week, so it's not easy. It's difficult to do things like go to the beach. We all have a great life, though. I know that Susan doesn't want to live in a normal house or flat in the city!

Speaker 4
I love visiting my sister Caroline and seeing her working – and seeing all the animals, of course. My favourite animal's Ned. He's a lovely old donkey. He sleeps a lot, but he's very friendly. Every day at about quarter to four, someone gives him a nice big apple. He loves it! When I visit the farm, I always ask if I can give it to him. They usually say yes! I would like to visit him every week, but I can only go to the farm once a month – something like that.

Speaker 5
I live in a big town, so it's great to come to a place like this. There's so much to see and do. It's my first visit actually, but I want to come back again. I don't really like animals usually, but everyone's so friendly, and you learn a lot about life on a farm. The food's not that bad either! I think it's a wonderful place!

Unit 3

Listening 1 & 2

Conversation 1

Assistant: Good morning. Can I help you?
Customer: Oh, hello. Yes. I'm looking for something for my friend. It's her birthday next week, and I'm trying to find something to give her.
Assistant: I see. I'm sure we've got something suitable. Do you have any ideas already?
Customer: You've got some nice pink skirts, and pink is my friend's favourite colour. I think she's already got one like this, though.
Assistant: We've got t-shirts in the same colour. Here's one.
Customer: Oh, that's nice. It's expensive, though.
Assistant: We're having a sale on t-shirts and jeans at the moment, so it's half price.
Customer: Oh. OK. Yes, this is perfect. Where do I pay?
Assistant: Just follow me, please.

Conversation 2

Customer: Excuse me. Are these Italian tomatoes?
Assistant: Erm no, I don't think so. Are you looking for Italian ones for a reason?
Customer: I want to make an Italian meal. It's got carrots and tomatoes in it. I've already got carrots and now I just need tomatoes. Oh, and some bananas for the dessert I'm making.
Assistant: We've got Italian tomatoes over here. They cost more than the others, but they're very good. Shall I put some in a bag for you?
Customer: Yes, please. And what about bananas?
Assistant: We're waiting for someone to bring our fruit. Try the supermarket next door. That's three pounds, please.
Customer: Here you are. Thanks.
Assistant: Thank you very much.

Conversation 3

Assistant: Yes, can I help you?
Customer: Maybe. I'm looking for a book called *The Pirate*. Do you have it?
Assistant: Yes, I'm sure we do. Let me check. Oh, it looks as if we don't have any left.
Customer: Oh, OK. Never mind. This one looks interesting. *Sun at Night*. What's it about?
Assistant: It's a love story. We're selling a lot of that book at the moment.
Customer: Right. Well, that's just the kind of book I like. And this one? *The Second Man*.
Assistant: It's an exciting story about two brothers. It's a children's book.
Customer: Oh, yes. I see that now. I don't have children, so I think I'll just take this book, then. Do I pay here?
Assistant: Yes, that's right.

Unit 4

Listening 1

Angela: Hi, everyone! Thanks for coming. So, the website is now online and I think it's looking really good.
Tony: Yeah, it looks great. I love your welcome message, Angela.
Angela: Thanks, Tony.
Tariq: I love the welcome poem! Who's the poet?
Angela: I am actually, Tariq!
Paula: And I love the interview with Mr Jennings. It's great!
Tariq: Thanks, Paula. It's fun asking Mr Jennings questions. He always tells the truth. I think!

Listening 2

Angela: Hi, everyone! Thanks for coming. So, the website is now online and I think it's looking really good.
Tony: Yeah, it looks great. I love your welcome message, Angela.
Angela: Thanks, Tony.

Tariq: I love the welcome poem! Who's the poet?
Angela: I am actually, Tariq!
Paula: And I love the interview with Mr Jennings. It's great!
Tariq: Thanks, Paula. It's fun asking Mr Jennings questions. He always tells the truth. I think!
Tony: Is he really 43?
Tariq: Yes, he is. He looks younger, though, doesn't he?
Paula: Yeah – he looks about 30 if you ask me!
Angela: Anyway, we need to talk about a few things. Tariq, we need another interview for next week.
Tariq: OK. Who's got some ideas?
Paula: How about Mrs Jennings? Then we'll see if Mr Jennings is telling the truth!
Angela: Good idea!
Tony: Yes, great idea.
Angela: OK, so Tariq – you talk to Mrs Jennings and ask her if she'll do an interview. I'm sure she'll say yes. Paula, we also need someone to write a review of the school concert.
Paula: When is it?
Angela: Check the calendar on the website!
Paula: Oh, yes! Here it is. Erm. It's on Friday.
Tony: What time does it start?
Paula: At eight thirty.
Angela: So, Paula, is that OK?
Paula: Yes, no problem. I'll be there so I can write the review.
Angela: Great. Thanks. Now, Tony. We need someone to write a news story about Mr Bennett. He's writing a book at the moment.
Tony: Is he? That's interesting! Right, I'll speak to him in the lunch break and ask him some questions. What's the book about? Why is he writing it? When will he finish? Those kinds of things.
Angela: Great. OK, that's enough for now. Let's meet again tomorrow. Thanks for coming!

Unit 5

Listening 1 & 2

Speaker 1
We went on a tour of South Africa last summer. We were there for two weeks, and we went everywhere! We were on the bus for three hours every day, and we made good friends with the other people on the tour. I took lots of photographs of the people and the animals. Some of the animals were very dangerous! The hotels weren't very good – they were expensive. I hope to go back to South Africa one day.

Speaker 2
It was a very long tour. We were there for about two weeks. I loved South Africa – there was so much to see and do – but it was just so hot! The bus was good, and there were some interesting people on the tour. The tour guide was really friendly and took us to interesting hotels. We did a lot of fun activities, and I had a good time.

Speaker 3
South Africa was fantastic! We went on a bus tour all round the country with about ten other people. We stayed in good hotels, and we had some delicious meals. Mum didn't like the weather, but I didn't mind. We were on the bus for hours every day, and that was a bit boring. The tour guide was funny, though! I was sad when we came back home.

Speaker 4
We went to South Africa last year. It was a good tour, and I had a nice time. I made friends with another girl. We had fun on the bus. We usually went to the back of the bus because the tour guide was at the front. He was boring, but he made the other people laugh. We took photos on our phones and sent them to friends at home.

Unit 6

Listening 1 & 2

So today, we're talking about strange and interesting animals. This first animal is called an aye-aye. He looks funny, doesn't he, with his big ears and long fingers. His teeth are similar to the teeth of animals like mice and rats. Do you know how he finds his food? He uses his teeth to make a hole in a tree. Then he pushes his long finger into the hole, and pulls insects out of the tree. He's actually a primate, so he's in the same animal family as monkeys … and humans like you and me! So, that's the aye-aye. This next one also looks very strange, doesn't it, with its big grey head, big nose and red mouth. It looks sad, doesn't it? It's called a blobfish, and they live in very very deep water near Australia. They're not very exciting really. Some animals run and jump and do fun things like that. The blobfish doesn't do anything. It doesn't even swim really. It just waits for some food to go by in the water and then opens its mouth and eats it.

Grammar 2, Exercise 1

Jake: Is there an elephant at the zoo?
Zak: Yes, there's a very big one!
Jake: Great! Is it an old elephant?
Zak: Yes, it's a sixty-year-old, grey, African bush elephant.
Jake: Wow! I hope it likes living in the zoo.
Zak: Yes, it's a happy elephant, don't worry!

Grammar 2, Exercise 2

Jake: What time does the zoo open?
Zak: At nine o'clock on weekdays and at half past eight on Saturday and Sunday.
Jake: Great! Let's go at the weekend, shall we? Saturday?
Zak: Sure. We can go by bus. I'll meet you at the bus stop on Harper Street.

Jake: How much does the bus ticket cost?
Zak: One euro.
Jake: That's OK. And how much does it cost to go to the zoo?
Zak: The zoo ticket costs about five euros, I think.
Jake: I'm happy to pay five euros to see the elephant!

Grammar 2, Exercise 3

Jake: Wow! This is a big zoo! Where does the elephant live?
Zak: It lives in an enormous garden over there. Let's go and see it.
Jake: I can see it! There it is! It IS a big elephant! It's eating breakfast.
Zak: Yes, they eat a lot of food. Did you know that elephants spend about 16 hours a day eating plants?
Jake: Wow! Cool!

Unit 7

Listening 1 & 2

Passenger: Excuse me. I wonder if you can help me. I'm catching a plane today, and I'm a little confused.
Assistant: Of course. Where are you travelling to?
Passenger: Egypt. It's a Premium Airlines flight. The number of the flight is … er … 217.
Assistant: Do you have a boarding pass? Let me have a look at it, and I'm sure we can help you.
Passenger: You see, it's my first time flying without my wife, and she usually has all the passports and knows where to go. My boarding pass is here. I think I need to go to 930. Is that right?
Assistant: Let me see. No, you see, here's your gate number. That's where your plane is. It's D13. That's down here on the left. Nine thirty is the time you need to be there. You need to be quick because it's five past nine now.
Passenger: Oh. Is that what 'gate closes' means?
Assistant: Yes. You can't get on the plane after that. It's usually twenty minutes before the plane leaves.
Passenger: OK. And my seat is 7F. Is that next to the window? I asked for a seat next to the window.
Assistant: Yes, I think it is. It's probably near the front of the plane.
Passenger: It doesn't matter. I just want to see the view.
Assistant: When you get on the plane, ask one of the flight attendants to help you find your seat.
Passenger: OK. Thank you. This way?
Assistant: That's right.

Unit 8

Listening 1 & 2

Speaker 1
I was walking down the street two or three days ago when I saw my friend Ron. He was riding a bike. He was a long way away, so I started shouting and waving. He didn't hear me, but he saw me waving, and came up to me. The problem was, it wasn't Ron! It was someone else. He looked like Ron, but it wasn't him! Luckily, he wasn't angry!

Speaker 2
My story happened last Saturday. I was shopping with my mum. We were in a clothes shop. I wanted my mum to see a shirt I liked, so I pointed at it. But as I moved my hand, I hit a man who was standing next to me! I said sorry and the man said it was OK, but I felt really silly!

Speaker 3
My dad was cooking at home last Sunday when someone knocked on the door. My dad opened the door, and it was the woman who lives next door. They shook hands – then my dad remembered that he had food all over his hands. The woman's hand was really dirty! They both laughed about it!

Speaker 4
My grandparents came to visit us about a month ago. We were sitting at the table having dinner, when my mum asked my grandpa if he wanted any more food. My grandpa didn't say yes because he was eating, so he nodded his head. But – and you won't believe this – when he nodded his head all his hair fell on the table! Really! All his hair! I didn't know, but my grandpa doesn't have real hair. He wears a wig on his head, and it fell off!

Speaker 5
I've got a similar story! My grandfather was staying with us for a few weeks. Every night, he kissed me goodnight before bed. One night, I went up to him and said 'Goodnight, Grandpa,' and he kissed me and started to say 'Goodnight.' But as he was saying goodnight, he had a problem with his teeth. He stopped talking and took all his teeth out in front of me! I didn't know it, but my grandfather doesn't have real teeth! It was very funny!

Unit 9

Listening 1 & 2

Liam: Mum, Dad, can I ask you something?
Mum: Of course, Liam. What is it?
Liam: Well, there's a party at Oscar's house on Saturday. It's for his birthday. Can I go?
Dad: I don't know, Liam. You've got a lot of homework at the moment, and a test next week.
Liam: But Dad, I can do my homework on Friday. And I can get ready for the test on Sunday.

Dad: Well, that's true …
Mum: I don't know, though, Liam. You're still very young, and we worry about you.
Liam: Oh, Mum! I'm nearly 13! I couldn't stay at Paul's house last month because you said I was too young! I'm growing up, and you can't see it! It's not fair!
Mum: OK, Liam. Don't get upset. We didn't say you can't go. What time is the party?
Liam: It starts at eight. And Paul's dad can bring me home. I asked him.
Dad: What time?
Liam: 11 o'clock. The party ends then. So what do you think? Please say yes.
Dad: Hmm … OK, but make sure you do your homework first.
Liam: OK, no problem. Thanks! Oh, one more thing.
Dad: What is it now?
Liam: Can I use your phone? I want to call Oscar to tell him!

Unit 10

Listening 1 & 2

Speaker 1
My best friend Toby's quite tall. He's taller than me. He's not fat at all. In fact, he's very slim. He's got short fair hair and blue eyes.

Speaker 2
Samantha – she's my best friend – has got long dark hair. She's not fat and she's not thin. She's just average! I'm heavier than her – she's actually quite light.

Speaker 3
My Uncle Colin is … well, how can I say this? He's quite fat. I think he needs to get more exercise! I don't know how heavy he is, but he's probably very heavy! Much heavier than my dad, his brother. He's got short hair – it's quite light – and he's quite tall too. He's a really nice person! I like him a lot.

Speaker 4
Carrie's my twin sister, but we look very different to each other. I'm tall and a bit fat, but Carrie's short and thin. I've got fair hair but Carrie's hair is much darker. It's strange, isn't it, that we're twins but we don't look alike at all!

Unit 11

Listening 1 & 2

Speaker 1
I've got a very busy week ahead. On Monday, I'm not going to do anything special, but on Tuesday I'm going to help Mum cook dinner. She's going to teach me a few things. We're going to see my grandparents this weekend, so I hope I can take some food for them. Before that, I'm going to play tennis on Wednesday and Thursday because I've got an important match next week.

Speaker 2
We haven't got school this week – we're on holiday – so I'm going to spend all day tomorrow lying on the beach! I try to do that as often as I can in the summer. After spending some time on the beach, I'm going to meet some of my friends from school. We like to see each other once a week and hear each other's news. In a few days, I'm going to go cycling. I need the exercise!

Speaker 3
This week, I'm going to do some fun things, and maybe some things that aren't so much fun! I'm going to write an email to my friend in China. She wrote to me last week and I need to reply to her. I'll do that tomorrow. Before I do that, though, I'm going to tidy my room this evening. My mum keeps asking me to do it, and I'm going to surprise her! I don't think I'm going to do anything special this weekend. I'm just going to stay in and watch a film.

Unit 12

Listening 1 & 2

Man: Lindsay, your next film's an action movie, is that right?
Lindsay: Yes, it's called *Run and Hide*, and we're starting filming next week.
Man: Is making a film like that hard work?
Lindsay: Well, it's great fun, of course but yes, it's very tiring. Next week for example we're doing six big action scenes in six days.
Man: Wow!
Lindsay: Yes, it's crazy, isn't it? On Monday, we're filming a scene in a forest. Some bad people are chasing me, and I climb a tree and my friends rescue me with a helicopter.
Man: Cool!
Lindsay: On Tuesday, we're going to the coast. I have a fight with a bad guy on the top of a cliff. Eventually, I push him off and he falls into the sea.
Man: That sounds fun!
Lindsay: Yes! Then on Wednesday, we're flying for three hours to a desert. In the scene, I'm lost, and I've got no food or water. In the end, my friends find me.
Man: By helicopter again?
Lindsay: No! On camels!
Man: Oh. And on Thursday?
Lindsay: On Thursday, we're filming in the countryside. We're starting off in a field with horses in. I have to catch and ride a horse to escape the bad guys. Then we're going to a lake, where there's a speedboat waiting for me. That should be fun!
Man: We all like fast boats!

Lindsay: Yes! Then on Friday, we're doing a scene where I have to ski down a mountain.
Man: Bad guys are chasing you, of course.
Lindsay: Of course!
Man: And on Saturday?
Lindsay: On Saturday, it's a day by the sea. We're going to a local beach and filming a scene where the bad guys fly over me in a small plane and try to shoot me!
Man: Well, it sounds very exciting – and very tiring. Lindsay, good luck with your new film. I can't wait to see it at the cinema!
Lindsay: Thanks a lot!

Unit 13

Listening 1 & 2

Speaker 1
We've raised money at school before, and we've done all sorts of things. Last year we walked a long way, which was very tiring because I don't normally do a lot of exercise. This year, it was my idea to invite people to the school and have a fair with games and food. I sold lemonade and lots of people liked it. I made 50 pounds!

Speaker 2
I wanted to do something for charity, but I didn't know what. I asked my mum and she suggested sitting in a bath of baked beans! I didn't like that idea, so I asked dad. He said his car was dirty and I could wash it for him! I got five pounds for doing that. And when the next door neighbour saw me, he asked me to do his too!

Speaker 3
Some friends and I decided to raise money for a local charity. We had the usual ideas, like going for a long walk or selling something. And there's a car wash in our neighbourhood and everyone has a clean car, so we couldn't do that. In the end, one of my friends had to go home to take his dog for a walk, and it gave us the idea. We offered to take people's dogs for a walk for money. It was really successful.

Speaker 4
This is a really good idea, and I've done it twice now. You say that you're going to walk a long way, like 20 miles. And you ask your relatives and your friends to give you money for every mile you do. Then when you finish you go and get the money from them. It's a great way to raise money for a charity. It can be tiring, but you know it's for charity.

Unit 14

Listening 1 & 2

Man: Excuse me. I wonder if you can help me. I'm new here and I think I'm lost. I don't know if I'm going the right way or I need to turn round. I'm trying to get here but I don't actually know where I am right now. I can't see any street names!
Woman: Let's have a look. Right. Well, we're here. This is the corner of Earth Street and Sun Road.
Man: Right. So, what's the best way to…
Woman: Well, I think the best way is to go down Earth Street until you get to the crossroads. Then turn left. Go straight ahead until you come to the museum. If you turn right into Mars Street, you'll see a supermarket on the right. Go past the supermarket and go straight on until you reach the theatre. Cross the road at the traffic lights, and go straight on. You'll see a shopping centre on your right. Go past the shopping centre and you'll see a big building on your left. That's where you want to go.
Man: Thank you very much.
Woman: You're welcome. Oh – and welcome to the Moon!

Songs

Units 1 & 2

LIFE ON THE FARM

The people who live in the town, they think the country's quiet.
I say to them, 'Well, come on down, and for a day just try it.'
My family has a farm, it's true. There's never time to play.
There's always lots of work to do. Here's what happens every day.

At five o'clock, my sister goes and brings in all the eggs.
And then my brother milks the cows and feeds the dog.
What's next?
At six o'clock, my uncle feeds the hungry hen and chicks.
My cousin feeds the pony next, and then it's half past six.

My nephew takes the sheep and lambs and makes sure they're all fed.
My great-grandmother feeds the donkey – he's the one called Ned.
The ducklings, puppies, kittens, too, their breakfast's nearly ready.
And then the calves all need their food. A quarter to eight already!

We never rest. We never stop. It's always just like that.
We never have a second to just sit and have a chat.
The country is a noisy place. My family life is wild.
Sometimes I think it's better to just be an only child!

Units 5 & 6

TRAVELLING AROUND THE WORLD

London … Tokyo … New York … Paris … Sydney!

She's taking a ferry, now she's taking a train
She's taking a taxi, now she's taking a plane
She's stuck in traffic but she's on her own
She's travelling around the world, all alone

She's in a New York carriage in Central Park
She's got a ticket to the opera after dark

She's in a capital city but she's on her own
She's travelling around the world, all alone

She's going round the world like a butterfly
She's eating up the sights like a crocodile
She's moving place to place like a goldfish in a bowl
She's living very simply like a mouse in a hole

Europe, Asia, Africa too
North and South America – to see the view
Millions of people, but she's on her own
She's travelling around the world, all alone

She's going round the world like a butterfly
She's eating up the sights like a crocodile
She's moving place to place like a goldfish in a bowl
She's living very simply like a mouse in a hole
She's going round the world like a butterfly
She's eating up the sights like a crocodile
She's moving place to place like a goldfish in a bowl
She's living very simply like a mouse in a hole

Units 9 & 10

JENNY'S ONLY THIRTEEN

Jenny's only thirteen, but she's growing up now.
Sometimes she's angry or scared.
She knows she shouldn't argue, or cry or frown,
But sometimes life isn't fair, oh, yeah.
Sometimes she says life isn't fair.

She's sorry that she hurt your feelings.
She's sorry for the time that it takes.
She's sorry if she didn't do things right.
She only did it by mistake, oh, yeah.
She only did it by mistake.

Jenny's only thirteen, and she tries to smile,
But sometimes she doesn't feel strong.
She tries to get permission to live her life,
They don't let her, and then it feels wrong, oh, yeah,
When they don't let her, then it feels wrong.

She's sorry that she shouted and screamed.
She's sorry for the words that she used.
She's sorry if sometimes she seems weak.
It's just that sometimes she's confused, oh, yeah.
It's just that sometimes Jenny's confused.

Units 13 & 14

TIME GOES ON

I've been rich and I've been poor
I haven't known the answer and I've been sure
I've wasted money and I've saved it too
If you want to hear what I've learnt well, then I'll tell you …

Every day, every week, every month, every year
Time goes on
Every week, every month, every year, every decade
Time goes on
You can't turn round and you can't turn back
You just go straight on down the railway track
Night follows day and day follows night
Just try to do your best and you'll be all right
Just try to do your best and you'll be all right

I've been poor and I've made money
Sometimes it rains, sometimes it's sunny
I've cried a lot, but laughed a lot too
If you want to hear what I've learnt well, then I'll tell you …

Every day, every week, every month, every year
Time goes on
Every week, every month, every year, every decade
Time goes on
You can't turn round and you can't turn back
You just go straight on down the railway track
Night follows day and day follows night
Just try to do your best and you'll be all right
Every day, every week, every month, every year
Time goes on
Every week, every month, every year, every decade
Time goes on
You can't turn round and you can't turn back
You just go straight on down the railway track
Night follows day and day follows night
Just try to do your best and you'll be all right
Just try to do your best and you'll feel all right
Just try to do your best and you'll be all right